"Most people plan their vacations better than they plan their lives. This book is a beautiful road map for anyone seeking a way out of feeling stuck in their life."
Mary Kay Ash
Mary Kay Cosmetics

"Some of the world's best thinking on self-esteem, productivity, and goal-setting . . . Original, fresh . . . It cannot fail to help the person who has become 'stuck' in the muck and mire of life."
Art Linkletter

"The secret to a successful, meaningful, and joyful life by combining the power of God with the power of a positive mind. They have shown us how we can meet our needs and find Life Plus."
Dr. Robert Schuller
Author of *Tough Times Never Last But Tough People Do!*

THE LIFE*PLUS PROGRAM FOR GETTING UNSTUCK

Jane and Robert Handly
With Pauline Neff

FAWCETT CREST • NEW YORK

A Fawcett Crest Book
Published by Ballantine Books
Copyright © 1989 by Robert Handly, Jane Handly, and Pauline
Neff

Library of Congress Catalog Card Number: 88-15781

ISBN 0-449-21828-7

This edition published by arrangement with Rawson Associates,
an Imprint of the Macmillan Publishing Company

Manufactured in the United States of America

First Ballantine Books Edition: May 1990

To my loving family—the ones who have sustained and supported me on my path to Life Plus:

Mother and Daddy
My son, Miles
My sister, Rebecca
My niece, Summer
My Aunt Margaret and Uncle George

—JANE HANDLY

To Marlane—my teacher, my friend, my beautiful sister. I love you.

—ROBERT HANDLY

Contents

Contents

Foreword

In the final chapter of this inspiring book, Jane and Bob Handly give six steps to use to "get unstuck" and start on the path to Life Plus. The first one is "Read this book through two times."

When I reached that point in the manuscript, this direction was unnecessary for me. Why? Because I had already gone over the book several times during my first reading. I didn't want to miss a word! I was completely captivated by this remarkable piece of work, and I continue to be. I will read it many times because there is so much in it that helps, inspires, and motivates me.

This book will do the same for you. It speaks to you about you. It gives you whatever you need to know to help you "get unstuck." It is—all at the same time—a love story, a guide to life fulfillment, a practical manual for understanding basic psychological principles, a spiritual handbook, a textbook on positive thinking and holistic living, and a constant personal companion from now on.

The Life Plus Program for Getting Unstuck has something in it for everyone. It comes very close to being all things to all people. You will eventually go through many copies of this valuable book—to give to family and friends and to replace those you will wear out through personal use.

This is a workbook. It is intensely personal. It was written just for you. It addresses itself to your needs and challenges, whatever they may be, helps you to understand them, and gives you techniques for solving them. It is comprehensive and thorough and, at the same time, it is breezy, informative, entertaining, understanding, and loving. It inspires you to know yourself and do something about yourself. Through the skillful and intriguing narration of personal experience and the relating of numerous case histories of others who have learned to "get unstuck," the authors pinpoint causes and help us help ourselves. They leave no doubt but that our experiences of life—good and bad, favorable and unfavorable—come from within ourselves.

By sharing the insights gained from their own personal challenges, and by giving us the self-change tools that they have developed and themselves use every day, Bob and Jane Handly show us how to free ourselves from the negative causes and effects of life and how to take charge of our own destiny. The authors' theme is *If we can do it, so can you.*

There is no need to wait any longer. Go ahead now with the great adventure of finding Life Plus. At the same time that you are reading your book, I will be reading mine—again.

—DONALD CURTIS, D.D.
    Author of *Your Thoughts Can Change Your Life*

Acknowledgments

We wish gratefully to acknowledge and thank those people who have helped us through our lives whenever we found ourselves stuck in various situations and circumstances. All of these people have been our teachers, and we appreciate the valuable lessons they have helped us learn.

For Jane:
Penny Kilpatrick, my dearest friend
Ellen Watson, my sister of heart
John McCormick, my gifted therapist
Penny Burd, for constant support

I give thanks to each for having been significant in helping me to learn about me and for being unafraid to love me honestly.

For Robert:
Mother and Daddy, who gave me unconditional love and lives to pattern after
Neva Davis and Jim Wilson, who taught me how to use my mind in a positive way
Cynthia Handly, whose constant support and friendship have sustained me in my times of need

Our deepest love and gratitude go to Pauline Neff, without whose gifted talent for hearing what's in our hearts as well as what comes out of our mouths this book would not be able to reach the hearts of our readers.

Dr. Donald and Dorothy Curtis continue to be our spiritual guides and teachers, not only in the way they talk but in the way they walk their talk.

The members and staff of the National Speakers Association, the most loving, hugging, sharing group on the planet, have given us fresh insight into our work.

Toni Sciarra and Eleanor Rawson have provided expert editorial advice and support of our ideas.

"I came that they may have life, and have it abundantly."
—JOHN 10:10

1

Are You Stuck?

Ask yourself if you feel stuck. Are you so worried about your children, your marriage, or your career that you can't think what you should do? Do you flounder in despair but tell yourself, "That's just the way it is"?

Think about whether you feel stuck because of the stress you feel over your appearance, your relationships with others, or your financial situation. Do you tell yourself, "I'm trying, but nothing seems to get any better"?

Consider whether you're feeling stuck because you are depressed over a divorce, the loss of a job, or chronic illness. Do you tell others, "I can't believe that this happened to me. Sometimes I just want to give up"?

Or are you feeling stuck without knowing exactly why? Do you find yourself asking, "How can I change when I can't identify the problem?"

Perhaps you look at neighbors, friends, or relatives and see that others are stuck, too. You want to help, but what can you do?

We have written this book because we want you to know that *you don't have to feel stuck*. Through our own struggles to overcome and through our combined careers as teachers, consultants to major national corporations, authors, and professional speakers, we have devised a simple, easy plan for getting unstuck. Now we travel over 100,000 miles each year helping people just like you get out of their ruts and make constructive changes in their lives. Many go on to achieve what we call Life Plus, a wonderful state of being in which *you never have to be stuck again, no matter what happens to you*. People who feel trapped by all kinds of painful circumstances are able to take action, to move out, to become excited, happy, and fulfilled.

Your Ten Basic Needs

Here is another pleasant surprise: You will actually *enjoy* the process of getting unstuck if you do it our way. How? By meeting one of your basic needs with each step of self-change.

We have discovered that while each of us is a unique individual, we all have the same ten basic needs. We all hunger for

- Self-esteem—the realization that we are beautiful inside
- Humor—the ability to laugh with ourselves and others
- Physical well-being—that great feeling that goes with fitness
- A positive mental attitude—thinking habits that permit us to be happy
- Productivity—knowing how to achieve everything that counts

- Self-discipline—the secret of setting goals and managing time
- The experience of beauty—the esthetic transcendence that brings joy
- A strong connection with the spiritual, intuitive side of ourselves—a belief in God and the inner power that accomplishes in us far more than we ever dreamed was possible
- Healthy relationships—open and honest closeness to important others
- The exchange of love—giving and receiving the force that generates life

If you are lacking in any of these ten basic human needs, your hunger continues. Your body, mind, and spirit react by causing you to feel stuck. You just don't know what to do, and if you did, you wouldn't feel like doing it. Using our plan, you can meet *all* of these basic human needs. Each time you follow a step that we outline, you feed yourself; your hunger goes away. Meeting your basic human needs is a way to reach out with loving action—to yourself!

A Journey to Fulfillment

Our plan for getting unstuck is simple, but it does require three things from you: You must be willing to set aside time to look at your life, to discover your unmet human needs, and then to follow the steps we outline. Both of us have learned through personal hardships and painful circumstances why it is important to meet our needs. If we had not, we would never have become the overcomers that we now are. We would still be stuck! It is important for you also to take time to know yourself at a deeper level, to master the tools we will give you to make changing easier, and then to take action.

Read the chapters on the ten basic needs carefully. Each includes a description of how it feels to be lacking in a particular need, with quizzes to identify whether you hunger to meet this need. If so, we show you how to use five basic POWER tools, which will enable you to

- Accept yourself as a person who deserves to meet your needs
- Obtain helpful information
- Learn to pray positively, as well as to affirm and visualize
- Risk making important changes in the way you live
- Reach out and help others along the way

We will inspire you with the stories of others who have overcome—stories of celebrities and leaders, of Biblical heroes, and of ordinary people who have done extraordinary things by meeting their needs. We will tell you how we overcame the stuckness that came with our own childhood tragedies—feelings of unworthiness, illnesses, loss, and divorce—and finally found Life Plus.

We offer our experience and hope that you will commit yourself to following our plan, getting unstuck, and going on to achieve Life Plus. We know you can do it!

2

What We Learned
About Getting Unstuck

We want to tell you about two people who found themselves in circumstances that made them *want* to give up, but who didn't. They could have said, "What's the use? I've tried. I've failed." But they didn't. Why? Because someone helped feed them when they hungered for the food of self-esteem, love, and a positive mental attitude. As they fed these basic human needs, they were strengthened enough to look at themselves and discover other human needs in which they were lacking—such needs as self-discipline, a sense of humor, the experience of beauty, and a deeper faith. They set goals to meet these needs. Their faith deepened, and they became productive human beings who hungered to help others. Finally, they found Life Plus.

The Woman Who Could
Have Been Stuck but Wasn't

The first person was a child back in the early fifties, before the development of the Salk polio vaccine. Each summer a terrible polio epidemic spread over the United States. Children could go to bed at night and wake up crippled in the morning. They could die within a few days. Almost everyone believed that the polio virus thrived in water. Desperate to protect their children from exposure to the disease, many parents forbade swimming in public pools. If it rained, they kept their children inside the house, fearing the virus might somehow lurk in puddles or even in the humid air.

One steaming hot August afternoon after a rainstorm in North Carolina, a mother told her two little girls that they could not walk in the cool woods across the street as they usually did. The four-year-old could not look for hopping toads and the seven-year-old could not fill her pockets with beautiful rocks. They would not be able to sit under the trees, watch the squirrels, and listen to their mother make up stories about them.

"Oh please, let us go into the woods," the girls begged. But their mother knew that only this morning another child on the street had succumbed to polio. She just couldn't take a chance.

"We'll play a game instead," she said. "We'll boil some big white eggs, and you can use your crayons to decorate the eggs to make them into people, animals, or any wonderful thing you want. And guess what! When you are through playing with them, you can eat them!"

Excited, the children ran to find their crayons. By the time the eggs had boiled, they knew exactly how they wanted their eggs to look. The four-year-old finished her first egg in two minutes flat.

"Mother, I want another egg," she exclaimed. Her mother was talking to a neighbor who had dropped by.

"Wait just a minute," Mother said. But the four-year-old couldn't wait. She ran to the kitchen, pulled a stool up to the stove, climbed up on it, and pulled the pot full of eggs in scalding hot water from the back of the stove. Reaching into the water to pick up an egg, she burned her hand so badly that she fell off the stool, pulling the pot of scalding water with her. Almost a half gallon spilled over the small child's body. She screamed, and her mother ran to her.

At the hospital, doctors warned the little girl's parents that the burns were so extensive that the child's vital body systems would be affected by the loss of fluid.

"You'd better pray. Pray hard," the doctor in charge told them. They did. People from their church prayed around the clock. The little girl almost died. She had many complications. Most of her teeth deteriorated, decayed, and fell out prematurely. Each week a nurse had to shave the little girl's head to cut down the chance of infection. But she lived!

The child's parents were so delighted when they could finally take her home that they didn't realize how others would feel about her ugly red scars, stubby hair, and toothless grin. The little girl didn't realize it, either. She was delighted the first time her parents took her to Sunday School. But not for long. Some of the children made fun of her. Some were frightened of her. No one played with her.

When the mother picked up the child, she saw the hurt and rejection in her eyes. She realized that while the burns had healed, the scars were deep. She took the sad child home, gathered the family around, looked into the child's eyes and said, "What's beautiful about you is on the inside."

Every day the mother told her child the same thing. When the child started to go to school, she still had scars and no teeth. Sometimes she would climb a tree to avoid playing with the other children, who made fun of her or ignored her. Many times the child came home from school crying, "I'm so ugly!" But the mother would put her arms around her and say, "Oh no, I love you, and you are beautiful. Look inside."

Whenever the child felt sorry for herself and wanted to mope in the corner, the mother got her up and involved. "All people are beautiful," her mother told her, "and that includes you."

What a wonderful legacy of self-esteem to instill in a child! When that little girl was ten years old, she came down with a form of bone cancer. She was lucky that the situation was detected early enough to be cured with massive doses of chemotherapy. She could have been stuck in self-pity, but her parents kept telling her that she was beautiful on the inside.

That little girl grew up to win a beauty pageant and became Miss Winston-Salem, North Carolina. Later she became a mother and a highly successful teacher. Despite the wonderful legacy of self-esteem, love, and faith given to her by her parents, however, she still had to struggle with life's disappointments. One of them was a divorce. She could have given up then, too, but she didn't. She came to realize that she had some basic human needs that were still unmet. She gave herself permission to take the steps that were necessary to meet those needs. Now she is happily remarried. She has a new and exciting career.

The woman in this story is none other than Jane Handly, the coauthor of this book. A professional speaker who has inspired thousands to get unstuck, Jane has appeared on national television shows like Robert Schuller's "Hour of Power." In addition, she is now co-owner of Life Plus, a Dallas-based company that provides motivational programs, speeches, and seminars to organizations, associations, and major companies nationwide. Because she developed a positive attitude despite her childhood tragedies, Jane can speak compellingly about human potential in the workplace and motivate her listeners to believe in themselves, attain loving relationships, and develop a strong faith.

"In speaking to others, I have come to realize that my childhood was no more traumatic than that of most of us. All of us have scars. I don't know whether or not I could see your scars as you could see mine if we were together. Scars sometimes are invisible when they come from worry, illness, or chaotic relationships, yet we all have them. Everyone we come in contact with has scars," Jane says.

"But here is the good news. No matter what your scars are, you *are* beautiful on the inside. When you believe that and act on it, your scars will not only bear witness to your pain, but also to your healing."

The Man Who Was Stuck and Didn't Know Why

One fall morning in 1978, a thirty-three-year-old man went to his Dallas office, propped his feet on his desk, and started reading *The Wall Street Journal*. It seemed that he had everything that anyone could possibly want—a loving wife and his own successful executive search firm. He golfed with his friends, took nice vacations, and enjoyed eating in fine restaurants. Secretly, however, this young man did not feel good about himself. If his firm was successful, it wasn't successful enough. It seemed to him that almost anyone could do anything better than he could. Others saw him as pleasant and outgoing. They didn't know about his worries and self-doubt. But his body did. It reacted with constant bouts of diarrhea, colitis, and a nervous stomach.

Suddenly, that morning as he read the *Journal*, his heart began to pound. Perspiration broke out on his forehead. His stomach churned and his mind went out of control with visions of death. He felt as if he were going to black out. He reached for the phone and quickly dialed his mother's number.

"Something terrible is happening to me. I feel as if I'm going to black out!" he gasped. Both he and his mother suspected the worst, since his father had recently died of a heart attack at age fifty-eight. She rushed to the office to take him to the doctor, but by the time they arrived, he was feeling calmed. The doctor's tests showed that nothing was wrong.

The young man did not know that he had had his first panic attack. He had never heard of panic attacks. His doctor hadn't either, so he told the young man he was probably working too hard. But soon there were more panic attacks. The doctor prescribed tranquilizers, which didn't help at all. In an effort to avoid the dreadful symptoms of panic, the young man stopped going to places where the attacks had occurred. But the attacks kept recurring, so often that at last he was housebound. If he so much as tried to step out the door to pick up the morning paper, he had a panic attack.

The young man could not explain to his wife what was wrong. She was sympathetic, but he nevertheless found himself stuck in a black depression. While his wife worked, he had to stay at home. His business was failing. They had no social life any more. Worst of all, the young man feared that he was going crazy, and he was terrified to talk about it. He began to think about suicide as the only way out.

Then one morning he read in the paper about a woman who had had the very same kind of strange attacks he had. The article said that she had agoraphobia, a fear of open spaces. After receiving help from a psychotherapist, she now lived a normal life.

The young man lost no time in going to the same psychotherapist, who taught him that agoraphobia was simply the body's response to overwhelming stress. It was a normal reaction—a "fight or flight" response to something that the body recognized as being dangerous. What was the danger that alarmed his body as he read *The Wall Street Journal*? Negative thoughts, worry, and self-doubts! Because he had not met his basic human needs for self-esteem, a positive mental attitude, and physical well-being, he unconsciously was sending messages to his body to pump adrenaline into his bloodstream and prepare his system to run away from or fight the inner enemy of dissatisfaction.

The psychotherapist explained that he couldn't remove the young man's stress, but he could teach him techniques to cope with it. The process involved self-discipline, positive thinking, and learning to love himself rather than criticize himself. The young man was diligent. Within six months he was healed. He could go everywhere and do anything he liked. He was so thrilled with this change that he decided he wanted next to meet his needs for physical well-being. He set goals for himself to stop drinking, to lose weight, and to become more physically fit. He attained them. He then set goals to give and receive love and to deepen his spiritual life. When he had met many of his needs, he had a transformation experience. He could feel a loving power in his life that was greater than his own.

The young man felt as if he were a completely different person from the one he was before he had panic attacks. He wanted others to know how beautiful life could be, so he embarked on a new career as a professional speaker, telling others how they could meet their needs and avoid stress and anxiety. He wrote two books, *Anxiety and Panic Attacks* and *Beyond Fear*, to explain in detail how to get over panic attacks and phobias of all kinds.

Although this young man had met many of his needs, the circumstances in his life continued to present him with many anxiety-producing situations. He got a divorce, turned forty, and had to deal with the stress of success in business and as a popular author. His first book sold so well that he (who had once been afraid of flying and public speaking) toured the United States and appeared on national TV programs like "Phil Donahue" and "Nightline."

The young man continued to give himself permission to meet his needs. He found an even deeper faith in God, a greater love for others. And yes, he found Jane, too, for the man whose story we tell is none other than Bob Handly.

"I know what it is to be stuck, because I had agoraphobia. But that's not the only way to get stuck. You can be stuck in a career or in a poor relationship. Sometimes you just feel stuck for no apparent reason at all. It's as if you can't move forward or get things together," Bob says.

"Now I know that agoraphobia is the best thing that ever happened to me, because if I hadn't had it, I would never have learned to meet all my human needs."

Our Promise to You

We are so happy with our Life Plus kind of existence that we want you to have it, too. We want you to know how to help yourself *and* others who are stuck. One of the joys of becoming unstuck is that you really and truly do want others to have happiness, too.

In the next chapter we will present our plan for helping you get unstuck. We don't know exactly what the results will be in your life if you follow our plan, but we do know that you will get out of your rut, whatever that might be. You may be surprised yourself at the wonderful things that happen to you as a result of getting unstuck.

So turn the page, read on, and pledge that you will take the time to meet your human needs. We promise you that the results will be good!

3

The Life Plus Program for Getting Unstuck

The idea for this book took shape one morning when we were praying for people who were troubled. One friend of ours was verging on ulcers because she couldn't deal with an eccentric mother. Another was in despair because her husband was hostile toward her no matter how hard she tried to please him. A businessman we knew was bored with his job but afraid to leave it. Other friends were in a state of distress because they didn't know what to do about problem children, a divorce, or financial problems.

All of these individuals were dysfunctional, and yes, very sad. No one felt fulfilled. Everyone bore painful scars. After praying for them, we began to discuss their individual situations.

At first it seemed to us that none of those for whom we prayed had caused their own problems. Someone near to them was wreaking havoc, or some outside event was disrupting their life. How easy it would be to think of them simply as victims of circumstances, we agreed—

except we knew that that kind of thinking never helps. Instead of *giving up*, they needed to *give out* whatever it took to get unstuck.

John Goddard, author of *Kayaks Down the Nile*, has been described as a present-day "Indiana Jones" because he has reached his goals of climbing the highest mountains and swimming the deepest seas. He says in his book that some of us wait so long for our ship to come in that our pier collapses. Whenever we feel stuck in apathy, depression, despair, anxiety, or fear, we need to stop playing the victim! Of course bad things happen. But we need to take responsibility for our reactions, turn our gaze outward, and make the changes that *will enable us to feel differently even if the circumstances remain the same*.

We, too, have had the experience of feeling stuck because of circumstances, and both of us have discovered that we had to change our attitudes in order to get unstuck. Jane remembers the time when she, her first husband, and her son, Miles, moved to a suburb of Dallas.

"I hated Texas," Jane says. "I wasn't ready mentally or spiritually to move from our little country house in Clemmons, North Carolina, to a big metropolitan area. I had always lived close to my parents. I had a network of loving friends and a successful career teaching school.

"For the first few weeks I felt that only my body had moved to Texas, while my mind remained in North Carolina. I called 'home'—North Carolina, that is—every day. Some days I called two or three times. I didn't get involved in my new community. All that mattered was counting the weeks until I could go 'home' for a visit.

"One day I called a lifelong friend of mine. She

listened to me dwell on my misery for as long as she could stand it. Finally she said, 'Jane, don't you think it would be helpful if you let your mind join your body in Texas?'

"I stood there thinking for a long, long time. I've always known that anyone who wants happiness has to be united in body, mind, and spirit. Now my friend was telling me that I had separated my body from my mind and spirit by about one thousand miles! Was I grateful for this revelation? No! I felt only anger. She was telling me that if I was unhappy, *I had to change*!

" 'You don't understand what it's like to be away from those you love,' I countered.

" 'I do understand that it's very hard and very sad. But I also know that the only thing that will make you happy is getting your body, mind, and spirit together,' she insisted.

"We talked a long time, and after we hung up, I decided she was right. I resolved to let my mind and spirit join my body and to go out and become aware of where I was in Texas. You see, I really hadn't *seen* the place or noticed the people. I was operating out of fear and anxiety and an unwillingness to risk walking next door and introducing myself. I hadn't tried to make friends. I hadn't asked where I could find a dry cleaner, a drug store, a good supermarket, a service station, or a church. No wonder I felt so alienated!

"When I became *accountable to myself for my own happiness*, I set definite goals to do all those things. While I was at it, I took a good, hard look at myself and the way I had been living. I had to admit that I really was a little tired of teaching school and that I wasn't happy in my marriage. I had many needs that were unfulfilled. Then I *let myself dream* that in Texas I could change all that. I *visualized* myself in a new career and a happy marriage, surrounded by wonderful friends. Finally, I *risked* going out and making contact with others. The amazing thing was that all the things I dreamed about came to me. When I took responsibility for fulfilling my needs, I did more than get unstuck. The circumstances were the same—I was still in Texas—but I found Life Plus even so."

How wonderful it would be, we decided, if all those for whom we prayed could have the same change of attitude that Jane had had. We knew that even though their circumstances might not change, *they* could. But they needed to stop letting apathy win, to stop waiting for something to happen.

The problem, we concluded, was that most people who feel stuck just don't realize that it's in their power to get unstuck. But we did. And we wanted to tell them. And that's how we happened to write this book.

Are You Stuck? The Life-Quality Quiz

Sometimes you know exactly why you're stuck. At other times you may feel dissatisfied without quite knowing why. Or you may think you know, but you don't see the whole picture. For instance, Jane knew that she was feeling depressed and lonely because she was forced to leave North Carolina. She didn't realize that she also had been feeling stuck in her career and marriage until she sat down and took a good, hard look at herself. She didn't realize that she had unmet needs.

If you are feeling stuck, the following Life-Quality Quiz will help you understand why. Please rate how you feel about the quality of the different areas of your life, which are listed below. Give yourself a 3 for "very satisfied," a 2 for "sometimes satisfied," a 1 for "rarely satisfied," and a 0 for "not at all satisfied."

		Satisfaction Rating
1.	Status of my career	3 2 1 0
2.	Relationship with my coworkers	– 3 2 1 0
3.	Relationship with my boss	3 2 1 0
4.	Relationship with my spouse or significant other	3 2 1 0
5.	Relationship with my children	3 2 1 0
6.	My ability to make friends	3 2 1 0
7.	Quality of my friendships	3 2 1 0
8.	Financial status	3 2 1 0
9.	Quality of activities I do in my free time	3 2 1 0
10.	Status of my health	3 2 1 0
11.	My feeling about myself	3 2 1 0
12.	My ability to communicate with others	3 2 1 0
13.	My feelings about others	3 2 1 0
14.	The way I manage my time	3 2 1 0
15.	My ability to risk trying new things	3 2 1 0
16.	My ability to laugh and enjoy myself	3 2 1 0
17.	My ability to react to others with love	3 2 1 0
18.	My ability to overcome losses in my life	3 2 1 0
19.	My relationship with God	3 2 1 0
20.	My feeling about my future	3 2 1 0

Now add up your score. If your total is below 20, you are badly stuck and need to move on. This book will show you how. If your total is between 20 and 35, you have many areas of life in which you are functioning below an optimal level, and the exercises in the next chapters can be of great help. If you rated between 35 and 45, you can still benefit from learning how to get unstuck. If you rated above 45, congratulations! You are probably feeling satisfied with your life, unless, of course, you scored a 1 or 0 in any one category. The categories in which you scored low will help you understand which you need to work on first.

Why Meeting Your Needs Will Help You Get Unstuck

As you can see by the categories listed in the Life-Quality Quiz, the human needs that we are talking about vary from those listed by psychologists such as Abraham H. Maslow. This often-quoted American psychologist suggested the existence of a hierarchy of needs that could be illustrated in the form of a pyramid. At the base of the pyramid (and most essential) were the physiological needs, such as hunger, thirst, and sufficient warmth. Above this came a layer representing the need for safety. At the next level were belongingness and love, and then came self-esteem. At the very top of the pyramid, in a very small area, was the need for self-actualization—the ability to be responsible for yourself and develop into the person you truly want to be. Maslow's theory was that you couldn't become self-actualized until you first met all the needs on the lower levels of the pyramid.

For the purposes of this book, we are going to assume that you have already met your physical needs. While you may not be able to dine each night on caviar and truffles, you are not starving. You may not live in a mansion, but you do have a place to sleep. If you are feeling apathetic, depressed, generally stuck, or if you scored low on the Life-Quality Quiz above, however, you may not have met your needs for belongingness, love, and self-esteem. We agree that those are very important needs.

Important also is the need for self-actualization, which is similar to what we call Life Plus. In this state, you take full responsibility for your own happiness, and you are able to take loving care of yourself, no matter what happens to you.

For us, however, Life Plus goes beyond self-actualization. We place the greatest emphasis on the spiritual dimension. When you have achieved Life Plus, you have God's sustaining power to carry you through the tough times and to enable you to love yourself and enjoy the happy times to their fullest.

How Bob Found Life Plus by Meeting His Needs

Bob describes how he found Life Plus in this way: "I first had to take responsibility for overcoming my ago-raphobia," he says. "For six months I worked very hard, desensitizing myself to my fear of going out into the public. I learned special techniques to relax my body and reprogram myself with visualizations and affirmations that I was calm rather than anxious. I forced myself to go out and do the things I feared and act *as if* I were calm. At the same time, I replaced my negative thinking with affirmations of my self-worth in order to develop a positive self-image and greater self-esteem. I soon found that I was able to leave the house, go to the office, and be with friends once again. I was so pleased with these results that I decided to set goals to improve myself in other ways.

"One of my goals was to become more spiritual. I didn't know how to do this, but I read books that told how others had sought and found this vital source of strength and wisdom. I set aside time each day to pray and meditate. I began to experience a wonderful feeling of oneness with God. Eventually I had what I called at the time a transformation experience. I was driving down the highway listening to self-improvement tapes, and suddenly I felt for the first time in my life that I really loved myself. I loved everyone else, too. I felt as if nothing would ever make me angry, impatient, frustrated, or fearful again. I felt completely transformed!

"This new way to live was so wonderful that I called it Life Plus. I soon discovered that it was no guarantee that circumstances around me would remain pleasant. With Life Plus, however, I didn't have to fall back into my old habits of negative thinking and reacting angrily to what others did. I could remain calm and in touch with my spiritual self no matter what happened. In fact, my spiritual awareness became stronger as time went by.

"Now I know that if I hadn't met my need to feel beautiful about myself from the inside out, and to gain healthy relationships with others and with God, I could have started having panic attacks again," Bob says.

If your car gets stuck in the mud, you know how to throw gravel under your tire to drive out of the rut and get moving. "Living Life Plus," as we call it, doesn't mean that you always will be driving down a well-paved highway. You're likely to encounter potholes and icy bridges. Another car may even crash into yours. That's why our goal is for you to do more than become self-actualized. We want you to *live Life Plus*, so that no matter what obstacles you meet, you will keep on going down life's highway with peace and contentment. You don't need to fear getting stuck once you know how to be an overcomer. That's why we discuss some needs that Maslow didn't list.

A Closer Look at the Ten
Most Important Human Needs

If you want to achieve Life Plus, we believe that you must satisfy the ten most important human needs. These are:

1. *The need to feel beautiful from the inside out.* God has given each of us special talents. But not all of us can accept our inner beauty. Like many others, you may lack confidence. You may not feel that you deserve success. You may be short on self-esteem. If you haven't met this need, you likely are spending a lot of time and energy putting yourself down, feeling inferior and powerless to change circumstances. You can rid yourself of these destructive feelings by learning to nurture yourself and accept the worthiness you already possess.

2. *The need to have a sense of humor.* Perhaps you've never thought of a funny bone as a human need. Without it, however, minor illnesses, anger, and depression are likely to make you feel stuck. If you don't have a sense of humor, you can develop one. You will enjoy doing it, too!

3. *The need to be ship-shape physically.* Anxiety, illnesses, weight problems, smoking, drinking, and other unhealthy habits can send your emotional thermometer below freezing. Then you're *frozen* stuck. Does just thinking about confronting your physical problems make you reach for a cookie, a cigarette, a martini, or tranquilizer? Don't! We'll show you a better way to meet the need for physical fitness.

4. *The need to get out of the prison of your thoughts.* It is all too easy to sabotage your achievements with

worry and negative thinking. When you use our technique of wide-angle focusing to see the positives in your life, you find that the world exists in living color rather than in black and white.

5. *The need to be productive*. If you lack a sense of purpose in life or if you are dissatisfied with your progress in your career, you may not be meeting your need to feel productive. Time management techniques are not the only answer to meeting this need. We will show you simple strategies for how ordinary people can achieve extraordinary results and how people who are a little out of the ordinary can invest their talents for spectacular payoffs.

6. *The need for self-discipline*. If your life is chaotic and fragmented or if you have tried to improve and failed, you may not have met your need for setting goals and "keeping on keeping on" until you attain them. We can show you how to set achievable goals and develop daily routines that make it easy to work on those goals.

7. *The need to experience beauty*. If you are bored and joyless and don't know why, you may not have met your need to enjoy the beauty in a sunset, in music, theater, dance, and drama, or the laughter of children. Contrary to what you might think, you can learn to enjoy them.

8. *The need for a personal relationship with God*. If you feel alone, hopeless and helpless, afraid of life or death, you may lack a close relationship with God. We can't meet this need for you, but we can tell you how we and others have met it and have found peace, harmony, and joy.

9. *The need for healthy relationships with others*. If you feel hurt and lonely, if you feel that others are cold or uncaring, you may need to learn how to develop healthy relationships. We show how to balance your responsibilities toward family, career, and yourself, and how to develop close ties to the people whom you deeply care about.

10. *The need to receive and give love*. Research shows that babies who are not cuddled and loved do not thrive and may die from marasmus. You must receive love and pass love on to others if you are to achieve Life Plus. We show you practical ways to do this.

The Story of Annie

Why do we say that having Life Plus is more than just being self-actualized? While speaking at a church mother–daughter banquet, Jane met a very special person who demonstrated the difference.

"I was telling the women how I had been burned as a child, as I often do to make the point that true beauty is within you. Suddenly I saw that all the women were beginning to cry. I thought, 'This story is not that sad. Hang on! It's going to have a good ending.' But they just kept weeping. So I stopped and asked, 'Is there something I need to know about?'

"About that time a woman walked into the back of the room. In her arms she carried a little child who looked to be about three years old. In fact, she was seven. Her name was Annie. She had a very rare genetic disease called Williams Syndrome. Her tiny body couldn't grow, and she had associated heart problems. She looked like a little pixie, with pretty, sparkly brown eyes and a chest that was too big for her tiny arms and legs.

"Someone brought Annie to me and put her in my arms. When I looked down at her, I noticed with a shock that she had been scalded over her body, exactly where I had. Her scars were very prominent. Then I realized why the women were all crying. Their hearts had been with that child throughout her painful ordeal.

"I was going to be dramatic, as speakers are prone to be. I was going to look into that little child's eyes and say what my mamma said to me. I was going to say, 'Annie, what's beautiful about you is on the inside.' But before I could do this, Annie looked up at me.

"'You're a purty lady!' she said. I couldn't say a word. My tears were rolling down my face. That worried Annie.

"'You want me to sing a song?' she asked. I put that little girl down on the floor, and with all her might she began to sing, 'Noah and his ark went splash.'

"As I watched that child sing, I thought, what joy she has! I thought about all my pointless worries, all my petty fears. 'Teachers come in all kinds of packages,' I reminded myself. 'Annie is neither the prisoner of her body nor of her thoughts. She *knows* she is beautiful inside. She gives and receives love, she enjoys singing, and she has a special relationship with God. The chances are that Annie will stop living one day soon. She just won't be there, but until she goes, she is certainly spreading joy.'"

Then Jane thought about something else. "If Annie were merely self-actualized, she would function despite her disabilities," she told herself. "But because she has Life Plus, she *enjoys* life and inspires others."

Is Life Plus for You?

You may be thinking, "Yes, I want Life Plus, too. I want to get unstuck and start spreading joy no matter what my circumstances are. But meeting those ten human needs sounds rather overwhelming. How can I do all that?"

First of all, you don't have to do it in a single day. We suggest these five steps:

- Read this book from beginning to end two times before starting to meet your needs.
- Buy a notebook in which you can practice the written exercises we will outline for you in the chapters that follow.
- Prioritize your needs. By reading this book you will be able to discover which need you most want to fulfill. Work on this one first. Then, when you have made progress, start working on the others.
- Practice the techniques that we will show you in the succeeding chapters. These will make it easy and enjoyable for you to meet your needs.
- Believe that *you can overcome being stuck*, whatever your problems may be.

Remember what Jesus said to the man lying crippled on a pallet at Bethzatha, the pool at the Sheep Gate in Jerusalem (John 5:2–9). People believed that the waters of the pool could heal at the moment when they began to ripple. However, only the first invalid to get into the moving waters could benefit. This man had waited sick and alone for thirty-eight years. He had been waiting for circumstances to change for almost four decades!

"Do you want to be healed?" Jesus asked. The man replied that he had no one to help him, so someone

else always got into the rippling waters first. Jesus ignored the man's evident desire to play the victim.

"Rise, take up your pallet, and walk," Jesus said. In
a flash, the man realized that God *wanted* to give him
the priceless gift of mobility. He needed only to take
action to overcome his disability. When he rose and
took up his pallet, he found to his great joy that he
could walk.

This is what we ask you to do, too. Believe that you
can become an overcomer, no matter what your circumstances. Begin to take action now.

4

The POWER Tools That Can Help You Meet Your Needs

We love the story about the two cows who were chewing their cuds one day when a milk truck passed by. On the side of the truck was a sign that read, "Our milk is the perfect food. It's pasteurized, homogenized, calcium-fortified, enriched with Vitamin D and full of nature's most valuable nutrients." One cow looked at the other and sighed, "Sometimes I sure feel inadequate, don't you?"

Perhaps after reading the last chapter, you are feeling somewhat inadequate, too. You want to get unstuck. But how do you take the first steps out of the rut?

From our own experience, we know one thing for sure. You don't get out of the rut without making changes. We have developed five techniques to make change come easier. Just as an engine and a winch enable a tow truck to haul an eighteen-wheeler out of a ditch, our five POWER tools can get you unstuck by simplifying the process of change.

Use the Five POWER Tools to Receive Your Blessings

1. **P**   *Pledge* to accept yourself as you are.
2. **O**   *Obtain* information relevant to your needs.
3. **W**   *Work* to master the techniques.
4. **E**   *Engage* in risk-taking.
5. **R**   *Reach out* to reinforce.

One young mother mired in car pools, career, and a life ruled by a ticking clock, said, "Whenever I'm in the midst of adversity, it's like being in a swamp surrounded by hungry alligators. People standing on the bank tell me that the experience can be a blessing if I will let it be. All I have to do is make some changes, they say, and then I will learn a wonderful lesson. But when I'm in the muddy water listening to the alligators roaring, their advice is not much comfort."

This young mother, like most of us, had a misconception of the difficulty of changing. She didn't realize that she only had to change *herself*, not her circumstances, to receive her blessings. She didn't realize that you can make big changes in your life by meeting your needs.

Has something happened to you that seems so overwhelming that you don't have the energy to make changes? We can't help but think that Charles Plumb, author of *I'm No Hero*, must have felt that way. Jane had the wonderful experience of meeting Charles and hearing him tell about being a U.S. fighter pilot in Vietnam. One day his plane was hit. As it fell toward the earth, it turned upside down, threatening to trap him inside. He managed to turn the plane around enough so that he could eject. He landed in enemy territory and was quickly captured. For the next six years his home was an eight-by-eight-foot cell with a dirt floor and a tin can for a toilet. His captors frequently tortured him by twisting his body with ropes.

"They would twist my body and I would think, 'I can take this much, I know I couldn't take any more,' and then they would twist me tighter. Then I would tell myself, 'I can take this much, but I don't think I can take any more,'" he said. Often he would be thrown back in his cell with torn muscles, and he would tell himself, "Well, I lived through that. I know I couldn't take any more." Somehow he survived each instance of torture.

One day Charles saw a wire appear beneath the bamboo wall of his cell and wiggle as if giving a signal. He watched the wire for several days before he had enough courage to pull on it. When he did, he found it came from another prisoner. Using the wire to signal letters of the alphabet, he began to ask questions. He discovered that two hundred other men were being brutalized just as he was.

When he was finally freed, Charles was flown to San Francisco, where he quickly tried to call his wife. He couldn't locate her. Then he called his father, who told him that his wife had left him. What a terrible blow after all that had happened to him!

"Come on home, son. It's a new day. Let's start fresh," his father said. What wonderful advice for Charles. What a liberating, positive sense of expectancy those words can conjure up for anyone! We think about them when we wake each morning: "It's a new day. Start fresh."

Charles could have been stuck in remembering the devastating six-and-a-half years in prison and the loss of his wife. He could have said, "I can't erase the bad memories or bring back my wife. I'm too exhausted and too scarred to make changes." Instead, he went home and started fresh by writing a book that has inspired countless others.

Few of us have been imprisoned and physically tortured, but many of us are anguished in spirit because of something that has happened to us. Yet each of us can start fresh—today. We can use the five POWER tools to meet our ten basic human needs with ease. We don't have to block out all the joy that awaits us.

Pledge to Accept Yourself as You Are —The First POWER Tool

If you are feeling stuck, remember that right now God is providing happiness, success, productivity, and good relationships for you. You can't experience all this joy, however, if *you* stand in the way. When you are stuck, it is as if you have spun threads of unhappiness to bind yourself inside a cocoon. The darkness there permits no dancing, walking, or breathing, not even a wink of the eye. While you are blocked from the world, you can't help but believe that this darkness is the way life is. Yet all you need to do to experience color, vibrancy, beauty, and fresh air is to pledge to break through those threads you have spun. You don't have to *create* the happiness and success. God has already done that. It's there waiting for you. You only have to change yourself in order to breathe, walk, dance, and celebrate.

The First POWER Tool will help you identify the changes you want to make in yourself to work toward Life Plus. It will also help you lovingly accept yourself as you are, *where* you are, rather than be stuck in blame of yourself or others.

Jane once attended a seminar in which the participants were paired off and asked to tell each other about some bad experience that had befallen them. When each couple had finished their stories, the instructor asked, "How many of you believed that your partner could not have done anything to prevent what happened to them?" Almost everyone raised a hand. The seminar leader then pointed out that in every case, the story-tellers could have avoided a negative ending to the story if they had accepted responsibility for themselves and taken action based on that sense of responsibility.

"The woman who was my partner told me about going with her husband to a downtown hotel at night to attend a meeting," Jane remembers. "As they walked to the place where they had parked their car, her husband was attacked and murdered. She was left a widow with five children to rear alone. I couldn't believe that she could have done anything to make her circumstances different, but after the leader encouraged my partner to think hard about what she could have done, she admitted that she and her husband had parked on a dimly lit street rather than pay a few dollars to park in the hotel parking lot. Furthermore, other people at the meeting had offered to walk with them to their car, but the couple was in a hurry to go home and didn't want to wait for them. I saw that she really *could* have done things differently."

The point of this exercise was not to make the sto-rytellers feel guilty because hindsight showed them that they had made a mistake. It was to help them see them-selves as they truly were so that they could *accept without guilt* their role in what happened, *stop blaming* other people and events, and *start fresh* for the future. Jane's partner, for instance, learned that in the past she had considered money and time more valuable than herself and her husband. She also had been something of a gambler, taking shortcuts that led nowhere rather than follow the long but certain path. In this case, the "gamble" had had tragic results. She had gambled away her husband's life because she did not consider herself worth spending a little time to wait for protection. She saw that this lack of regard for herself stemmed from low self-esteem. Rather than stay stuck in self-blame or blame of others, she made her number one goal to meet her need for feeling beautiful from the inside out.

An Exercise for Using the First POWER Tool

Set aside a section in your notebook to work on mastering POWER Tool Number One. First describe a situation that weighs heavily on your mind. Perhaps you see your problem as a husband who acts as if he doesn't love you even though you try your best to please him. Perhaps you believe your problem is a smoking habit that you can't get rid of because you fear that you'll gain weight if you give up cigarettes. Perhaps you feel victimized by an abusive boss in a job you are afraid to leave.

Now ask yourself:

- What is really true about this situation?
- Could you have done anything in the past to prevent the problem?
- Can you do anything now?
- What feelings about yourself stand in your way?

Your answers to the above questions will help you decide in later chapters which human needs you should work to fulfill first. If you see that you have made past mistakes or that you are doing things that prevent your getting unstuck, take a moment now to realize that you have been doing the best that you know how to do.

Accept yourself as you are, *but pledge to make changes*.
Write out some affirmations about yourself, such as:

- It is perfectly acceptable for me to have feelings of
  _____about _____ .
- I accept myself as a person of worth even though I
  have made mistakes.
- I can choose to change habits that stand in the way
  of my happiness.

Alcoholics Anonymous' famous Twelve Steps have
helped many people get unstuck from a life destroyed
by chemical substances. The first step is "We admitted
we were powerless over alcohol—that our lives had
become unmanageable." Being powerless may sound
like a reversal of our advice to be responsible for yourself, to unblock and enjoy what God has provided, but
it isn't. In order to recover, alcoholics must first see
themselves as they truly are—as persons who cannot
drink without ruining their lives. Once they recognize
their addictive nature as the "enemy," they can pledge
to change by giving up alcohol and finding a Higher
Power to help them stay sober.

We know from experience that amazing things happen to us as a couple when each of us becomes willing
to accept ourselves as we are. Like all couples, we have
our disagreements. When we do, it would be easy to
dig in our heels and insist that the other person needs
to change first. We have found that when each of us is
willing to take a hard look at ourselves, to accept what's
there and be open to change, then somehow a spirit of
harmony comes into our relationship and creates a
greater intelligence for both of us. We believe that God
becomes available to us and through us, around us, and
everywhere. Then we are free of resentments, blame,

and anger. We like to discuss disagreements first thing in the morning during our mutual prayer time, because God's love helps us accept the things about ourselves that we don't like.

When our dog, Duffy, died, we had a disagreement over whether we would get another pet. At first Bob said he did not want the responsibility of caring for another animal. We discussed our differences and prayed about it. Over a period of about a month, Bob began to see that he missed having a loving pet. After he agreed to buy one, we then disagreed about what kind of pet to get! Jane preferred a cat; Bob wanted a dog. Each morning we continued to talk about it and to pray that we would have patience with each other. Then Jane visited the local pet store. She saw a soft, cuddly golden retriever puppy with big brown eyes that completely won her heart. But when she told Bob about it, Bob was aghast. He had never had a big dog, and he didn't think he would like one. We continued to pray. Finally, Bob visited the pet store and saw the puppy. He couldn't help but admit that she was a delight. We bought her that day, brought her home, and now Sunny is a most important member of our family.

Jesus promised us that where two or more of us were together in his name, he would be there with us. So whether you're trying to eliminate disharmony with a mate or a friend, it doesn't matter. In the presence of God, you can see yourself as you really are, accept the fact that you are that way, and then go on to receive God's wonderful love. You'll be amazed how liberated you will feel. Ideas for getting unstuck will come to you.

Some people have a real blind spot when it comes to seeing the beautiful things about themselves. They focus on every wart and every failure as a parent, spouse, or employee, believing that they are so bad or wrong that they can't be forgiven. Remember that love and beauty are available for all of us. They are like a big umbrella, opened to shelter anyone and everyone. If you have a hard time believing that, then you will want to meet your needs for finding a personal relationship with God and for feeling beautiful on the inside so that you can believe the good news.

Obtain Information Relevant to Your Needs —The Second POWER Tool

Before Bob found out what agoraphobia was, he feared that each panic attack might kill him. When the psychotherapist told him that panic was the body's natural fight-or-flight reaction to sudden danger, he was much relieved. If his "illness" had a name, he knew he could find information that would help him recover. His first source of information was the psychotherapist who taught him that his body was especially sensitive to stress and that his negative thinking made him even more susceptible to panic attacks.

Seeing and accepting his mind and body as they truly were, he began to search out self-help books and experts' advice on how to develop a more positive attitude. He took courses in how to relax his body. Eventually he joined the Phobia Society of America, which gave him access to professionals from all over the United States who had special knowledge about phobias and panic attacks. By obtaining this information, Bob found ways to meet his needs for self-esteem, a positive attitude, self-discipline, healthy relationships, and getting and giving love. The changes he made in himself resulted in his complete recovery from a phobia that many experts at that time considered a chronic condition.

Keep in mind that your ultimate destination is not only to get unstuck, but to find Life Plus. If you had a road map that showed you the way, this book would be the first signpost leading to your destination. By reading it, you are already using the Second POWER Tool. Be aware, however, that there are many other signposts to help you on your way. In each of the chapters on the ten basic human needs, we will suggest further sources of information. Be willing to follow avenues and byways that you would never have thought to explore. You will find a destination that is more pleasant than you ever expected.

Work to Master the Techniques —The Third POWER Tool

The Third POWER Tool involves using visualizations, affirmations, and goal-setting to master the technique of positive prayer. You've probably heard over and over the advice, "Pray, asking as if you have already received." By contrast, most of us pray for solutions, and the minute we stop praying we go back to worrying about whether God will fill our requests. Lacking faith, we just don't believe that we have changed. Since we don't believe it, we *haven't* changed.

That is not the way to pray if you want to change yourself. Instead, use *the gift of positive prayer. Know that the minute your prayer is over, you are already changed*. How is this possible? Because God has promised to give you good things. "Whatever you ask in prayer, believe that you receive it, and you will," Jesus said (Mark 11:24). When you ask God to change yourself for the better, he grants your request. Your responsibility is simply to realize that he has already done it.

One way you can do that is to use *affirmations*. These are statements to yourself that you already are the way you want to be.

The Bible is full of affirmations: "The Lord is my light and my salvation; whom shall I fear? The Lord is the stronghold of my life; of whom shall I be afraid?" wrote King David in Psalm 27. We can well imagine David changing from fearful to ferocious as he repeated these words while facing hordes of spear-brandishing Philistines.

"Though a host encamp against me, my heart shall not fear; though war arise against me, yet I will be confident," David continued. We can imagine that these affirmations helped David also battle the *inner* forces that made him feel stuck. During his tumultuous lifetime, David had reason to feel victimized, for his own king, Saul, tried to kill him many times. After David became king, his beloved son Absalom led an army against him. David may also have used such affirmations to deal with guilty feelings after he placed Uriah the Hittite in the front lines of battle to be slain so that he could marry Uriah's wife, Bathsheba.

You can repeat the many affirmations in the Bible or in other inspiring literature, or you can make up your own. Say them when you want to change. Repeat them while you are praying and you will feel yourself getting unstuck. If you feel unable to provide for your own happiness, affirm, "I am perfectly capable of making changes in my life." If you are feeling unloved, affirm, "God loves me and made me in his image." Affirmations are always *positive* and in the *present tense*. Never use negatives, such as "I am *not* going to feel dull and boring any more." Word your affirmation, "I enjoy

having a good time and I have a keen sense of humor."
This kind of affirmation will change your frown to a
smile.

Another technique to master is *visualization*, which
is a controlled kind of daydream. Using visualization,
you see yourself as if you were a character in a movie,
*acting the way you want to be rather than the way you
fear you are*. Visualizations are most effective when you
make use of all the five senses. Hear, see, feel, smell,
and touch whatever is in your movie.

For instance, if you are feeling unattractive, try sitting
in an easy chair, closing your eyes, taking a few deep
breaths, and then starting to pray. Begin to visualize
yourself at a dinner party being given in your honor.
All the people you most love are dining with you. See
their smiling faces around the table. The food (your
favorite dish) tastes delicious. The music you most like
is playing in the background and you are wearing beautiful clothes that caress your body with their softness.
Everyone looks at you in a loving manner, and you
return their affection. At the same time that you are
playing this movie, affirm, "I am a child of God, made
in his image." Thank God for his love and end your
prayer. You will be amazed at how much more attractive you feel.

Still another technique you can use is *goal-setting*.
Reflect on what you discovered about yourself when
you saw yourself as you truly were. Then reframe those
conclusions into positive goals. For instance, if you saw
that you were feeling stuck because you thought you
had to please someone else and couldn't do what you
really wanted to do, use your notebook to write down
the goals that will help you take responsibility for
yourself. Like affirmations and visualizations, goals
should be positive statements. You might write, "My

goal is to take responsibility for my own happiness by
___(date)___." Then write out the action steps that will
fulfill your need. By setting goals, you will know what
to pray for.

We'll have much more to say about how to make
goals effective in chapter 10, when we discuss meeting
the need for self-discipline. Right now, you need to
think only about establishing your long-term goals and
affirming your right to reach them.

An Exercise to Master the Techniques

The techniques of the Third POWER Tool are so
valuable that it is worth taking time out to practice
them. Think of a relatively minor situation that makes
you feel stuck. For instance, perhaps you are feeling
angry at yourself because you won't confront your
spouse whenever he unfairly criticizes you. Or let's say
you feel frustrated because you must write a report at
the office and you just can't seem to get started. Or
perhaps you are feeling pressured because your daughter wants you to wash and iron a blouse when you
don't have time, and you can't say no, even though
you know she could do it herself. Or perhaps you just
can't pass up the doughnuts that everyone else eats at
coffee breaks, even though you know you are overweight.

Head a sheet in your notebook, "Using the Techniques." Then make a subheading titled "Goals."

Write "My goal is _____." Fill in the
details. Your goal may be "to confront my husband
when he criticizes me unfairly." Or, "to write my report." Or, "to say no to my daughter." Or, "to stay
away from the doughnuts at coffee break." In phrasing
your goal, ask yourself these questions:

- Is it positive?
- Is my goal to change myself rather than others?

Next, make a subheading titled "Affirmations." Then write five affirmations about yourself. In phrasing your affirmations, ask yourself these questions:

- What have I felt was "impossible" to change?
- What could I change about myself that would make me feel unstuck even though the circumstances don't change?

Using the answers to these questions, phrase them as affirmations. Make them positive and in the present tense. For instance, you might write, "I am a worthy person. I am able to speak up when my husband criticizes me. I am able to say that I am pretty smart. I love myself. I like to nurture my self-worth."

Next, write out a visualization to use the next time you pray. Picture a scene in which you are taking actions that will cause you to change. Should you see yourself and others smiling and enjoying the situation? Should the people in your movie be expressing calm, comfort, or even celebration? Should you paint the scene in sparkling colors or serene blues and greens? Will you hear a Sousa march or a Chopin nocturne? How can the textures of your clothing and the furnishings enhance the mood you want to create?

For instance, you might create a visualization in which you are working on your report while seated in a chair made of a cloudlike substance. You hear the gentle splashing of a quiet fountain and your favorite music. From time to time coworkers, dressed in beautiful shades of blue and silver, bring you brilliant ideas along with your favorite food. They are smiling and helpful. As your fingers caress the computer keyboard, your report appears effortlessly on the screen and your coworkers applaud. You feel proud and happy.

Review your affirmations, the visualization, and your goals every morning when you first get up and immediately before you go to bed. Take a few minutes every couple of hours and repeat the affirmations throughout the day. Use the affirmations and visualizations when you are praying.

Engage in Risk-Taking
—The Fourth POWER Tool

When Bob was getting over his agoraphobia, he learned that the only way to improve was to practice what psychologists call desensitization. "I had to expose myself to the very thing I most feared—leaving my home—in order to improve. Each time I forced myself to leave the security of my house, my body became accustomed to dealing with the feelings of fear that caused the attacks. Eventually my body recognized that it was safe for me to leave home," Bob says.

"Each time I ventured out, I knew that I was risking a panic attack. But because I had used the Second POWER Tool—that of obtaining information—I also knew that if I had an attack, it wasn't going to kill me. It didn't mean that I had failed. Trying and failing and trying again was simply the process of growth.

"By risking having a panic attack (and not berating myself for it when I did have one), I completely recovered from agoraphobia. Now I know that risking is a very important step in making changes of any kind. Without taking risks, nothing happens."

We've already talked about the futility of praying in a positive manner and then, the minute you stop praying, starting to worry that God won't give you what you ask. Risking is having faith. It means going out and doing the things you would do if you had been changed, *even if you don't feel that you are changed*. Risking is having so much trust that you *act as if* you are the way you have prayed to be. Whenever Jesus healed people, he always told them that it was their faith that had made them well.

Right now, answer the following questions and then write in your notebook three ways to risk demonstrating that God is answering your prayers:

- What am I asking God to change about myself?
- What can I do to act as if I am the way I have prayed to be?
- Who will cause the change to come about?

Reach Out to Reinforce —The Fifth POWER Tool

In his Sermon on the Mount, Jesus said that we should not be anxious people, worrying about what we would drink, eat, or wear. "Seek first his kingdom and his righteousness, and all these things shall be yours as well," he promised (Matthew 6:33). We believe that Jesus was saying that we don't have to be stuck in worrying about anything.

What does it mean to seek God's kingdom? To us, it means recognizing that divine spark within us and letting it reach out to others with love and concern.

The Fifth POWER Tool enables you to *maintain* the changes that positive prayer and risk-taking have achieved. When you reach out to others, when you see how people respond to your reaching out, you just *can't* feel apathetic, angry, or depressed. Both of us seek creative ways to reach out to others, not only because we want to, but also because we know that doing so will keep us out of ruts. We feel fortunate that our seminars and books enable us to help so many people. (And there is always the possibility that someone will reach out right back to us—just as Annie did in chapter 3—and rekindle us!) We seek also to reach out to all with whom we come in contact. We consciously try to do this with at least one person each day.

God's wonderful gift to those of us who have had tragedies and troubles is that we in turn are able to reach out in a big way. At a positive thinking seminar we heard Og Mandino tell about his recovery from alcoholism. Without this painful experience, would he be as able to inspire positive thinking in others through his many books and lectures? We've heard Art Linkletter tell how his daughter, Diane, killed herself while under the influence of drugs. Because of this tragedy, he has devoted time, energy, and money to educate legislators, public officials, and average citizens to the problems and causes of drug abuse. At another time, we heard Dr. Robert Schuller tell how his wife's mastectomy and his daughter's loss of a leg in an accident enabled him to identify with the problems of those to whom he ministers. In our opinion, all of these individuals are seeking God's kingdom before focusing on their worries. Consequently, they are able to reach out to others in wonderful ways. Their lives have been greatly enriched, just as Jesus promised.

Open your notebook and head one page, "My Reach-Out Goals." On the left-hand side, head a column, "Date." Head the next column, "Person I will reach out to." Then, in the remaining space, write a heading that says, "How I Will Reach Out." Each day, think of a person to whom you will reach out. Fill in the date, the name, and the action you will take. A good time to do this is after your prayer or in the morning after you have reviewed your goals and affirmations.

Right now, take a moment to write out the ways that you will begin today to reach out to another. It doesn't have to be anything world-shaking. You could write a comforting letter, bake someone a cake, or call someone and tell them you love them. As you do these things, you will feel rewarded with greater peace of mind.

Master the POWER Tools

These tools are designed to serve you in meeting your needs. Remember: they are tools of power. They will make it easy for you to find Life Plus.

In the next ten chapters we will show you how you can use the POWER tools to meet all of the ten basic human needs. You will be surprised at the ease with which you will be able to do many things that you have never done before. We have found in our own lives that, once we get out of our own way and work *lovingly* with ourselves, the results can be nothing short of miraculous!

5

Becoming Beautiful from the Inside Out —The First Human Need

Back in the 1920's, when oil derricks were sprouting up over Texas like bluebonnets, geologists from several major oil companies considered drilling in Rusk County, in the eastern part of the state. Highly qualified geologists took core samples from several hundred feet below the earth, tested them, and declared the land worthless. If there was any oil in Rusk County, the geologists warned, it was so scanty that it wouldn't pay the costs of drilling.

That was not the opinion of C. M. (Dad) Joiner, a colorful Texas "wildcatter." According to Herbert Gambrell's classic *A Pictorial History of Texas*, Joiner gambled everything he owned on the hunch that Rusk County did hold valuable oil deposits. He leased the "worthless" East Texas land and brought in his first well in October 1930. Within a month, five thousand other wildcatters were swarming around nearby Kilgore. Photos taken in July 1931 show the amazing results: eleven hundred derricks crowded against each other in front yards and along streets within Kilgore alone! After less than a quarter of a century, the wells drilled throughout the 200,000 square miles of this sensational East Texas oil field produced three billion barrels of black gold. These giant pools of petroleum had lain buried in the earth for eons, but despite all their education and sophisticated methods, the geologists had not believed it.

Are you looking at yourself and refusing to believe that you are beautiful inside? Have denigrating statements others made about you in your childhood and adolescence "educated" you to view yourself in negative terms? Your value surpasses that of all the black gold in all the oil wells in Texas, but you may not believe it. Like the geologists who failed to recognize the signs of a lucrative oil field, you may be considering the wrong kind of information about yourself.

Without the feeling that you are beautiful from the inside out, you will find it hard to meet any of your other needs. That's why we have placed it first. Even though it is crucial, however, it doesn't have to be difficult to meet. The POWER tools make it easy to change faulty feelings about yourself.

The "Who Are You?" Quiz

Since the First POWER Tool is to accept yourself as you are, take a few moments to think about who you are. Then get your notebook and write six sentences to describe yourself. Don't read any further. Just write.

Now look at what you have written. Do your sentences really describe *you*? Or do they describe your relationship to others, to your possessions, to your career, or to your successes or failures? If so, you are defining yourself by what you or others have done or said about you rather than by what you are: a child of God, created with your own unique gifts, loved by God and therefore of great worth. Knowing that you are beautiful inside is a powerful force for getting you unstuck from any problem.

Studying the Self Words

Five qualities that will help you accept your inner beauty are:

- Self-worth
- Self-esteem
- Self-love
- Self-confidence
- A positive self-image

We call these the self words. Many people confuse their meanings, so let's define them right here.

Self-worth is the value that God gave you as a present when you were born. You don't have to earn it. It's a gift. If you don't feel worthy, you might catch yourself saying things like "Even though I disagree with my friend's opinions on politics, I wouldn't dream of telling him I feel differently," or "It's no wonder I haven't gotten a promotion—I always make mistakes," or "I can buy clothes for the kids or for my husband, but it seems like an indulgence to spend money on myself."

Self-esteem is the recognition of your self-worth. When you believe unshakeably in your inherent worth, you have good self-esteem. When you think you have to earn it and have fallen short, then you have poor self-esteem. You can spot poor self-esteem in yourself when you hear yourself saying things like "My son is smoking marijuana and it's all my fault," or "I'd like to take some courses to advance in my career, but it's not fair to ask my family to make the sacrifice," or "Thanks for the compliment, but it's really not true." When you recognize that you are beautiful from the inside out, no one but you yourself can take away this beauty.

Self-love is the regard you have for your own happiness. It is accepting yourself as you truly are, even when you make mistakes, and still giving yourself permission to enjoy all the wonderful gifts that life holds. You are lacking in self-love if you tell yourself, "I didn't study as much as I should have in college, so now I'll just have to pay for it," or "I'd like to take a vacation, but somehow I never find the time," or "As soon as this crunch at work is over, I'll attend to my relationship with my spouse/children/family." With self-love, you can nurture yourself even when you've failed to do whatever you wanted. You can tell yourself that you deserve to have good things in life—from a hot bath to a healthy diet to a loving relationship.

Self-confidence means having a basic trust in your ability to do whatever you want to do. You are lacking in self-confidence when you say, "The last time I tried to make a speech I got so nervous that I'm never going to speak before an audience again," or "It's easier to go to a party alone than to ask a date and risk being turned down," or "I hate my job, but I doubt that I could get anything better." You *earn* self-confidence by risking small things, succeeding, and then using the good feelings that result to go on and risk greater things. Each success you earn increases your self-confidence.

Self-image is your concept of who you are, based on how you have interpreted the things that happened to you as a child. If you believe that you did things in your childhood or adolescence for which you can never be forgiven, you may develop a poor self-image. When you become an adult, a constant, nagging sense of guilt may cause you to feel stuck. If instead you see yourself as a normal human being who is basically good but sometimes makes mistakes for which you *can* be forgiven, you develop a positive self-image. As an adult you will be able to recognize your humanity and the ups and downs of life as natural things. When you find yourself in trying circumstances, you can get unstuck.

If you don't recognize your self-worth or if you lack self-esteem, self-love, self-confidence, or a good self-image, don't tell yourself that your personality is locked in place and that you'll never change. When you meet the need to feel beautiful from the inside out, you will change. You will suddenly find that you can feel good about yourself.

When George Leonard wrote *Transformation* in 1972, he predicted such a radical improvement in human perceiving, feeling, and being that the change could only be called a "transformation." Westerners would stop living for the purpose of consuming and competing, he said. Instead, they would value themselves as human beings, relating at the level of the soul to their innate self-worth, to other people, and to the earth.

When Jane had the opportunity to sit with Leonard around a dinner table, she heard him say, "All steel can be melted down, and so can you." We agree that you can be transformed, but you don't need to wait for society to change in order to accept your worthiness and be confident. You can make the decision to be an overcomer now!

Answers to Your Questions

Look again at the six sentences you used to describe yourself.

Did you describe yourself as the husband or wife or parent or child of someone else? If so, you are attempting to bolster your *self-worth* by attaching yourself to the identity of other people. Remember, you don't have to do that, because you were born with self-worth. You only have to *recognize* that this gift is yours. You don't need to link yourself to anyone else's identity in order to feel worthy.

A friend whom we'll call Abbie was so distraught over the actions of members of her family that she couldn't function the way she wanted to. She had a teen-aged daughter who had run away, a son who was angry and withdrawn, and a husband who had lost his job.

"What am I going to do to help my husband and my children? I'm so worried I can't think," she told us. Abbie was floundering because she associated her self-worth with what she saw as the worthiness (or lack of it) of others. When *they* fell short, *she* felt like a failure and was unable to take constructive action. She told herself that if she had done such a poor job as a wife and mother, she didn't deserve to have a good life or feel good about herself. When she learned to recognize that she was a person of worth *regardless* of what others did, Abbie felt good enough about herself to find a job and learn parenting skills. Even though all her problems didn't go away, she got unstuck.

Some people do just the opposite. They sell themselves short because their relatives are big achievers. "I'll never be able to do the things they have done," they tell themselves. If you depend on the success of others to define your self-worth, you are failing to recognize what God has done for you.

Did you describe your home, your car, or any other items rather than yourself? If so, you may be depending on material things to bolster your *self-esteem*. You are not your possessions. No matter how poor you may be, you yourself are of infinite worth. Jesus said, "Look at the birds of the air: they neither sow nor reap nor gather into barns, and yet your heavenly Father feeds them. Are you not of more value than they?"(Matthew 6:26).

Jane's mother, Rachel Carter, learned early in life how stuck you can feel when your self-esteem is tied into the kind of clothes you wear. When she was seven, her father attended an auction given by a store that was going out of business. He came home with a large box full of shoes. Rachel's mother looked through them and exclaimed, "Oh look, here's a pair of high-top button shoes just like the kind I wore when I was a little girl. Rachel, you ought to wear them to school tomorrow." Even though Rachel's mother had not *required* her to wear the shoes, Rachel *thought* that she had. Though she considered the shoes tacky, she wore them the next day. At school she was terribly embarrassed. All day she sat at her desk with her feet drawn up underneath her, so that no one would see those awful shoes. During recess, she stayed at her desk. She could see her classmates outside pumping water from the well. Her mouth was as dry as a piece of sandpaper, but she didn't budge. That afternoon, when the teacher asked her to recite a poem, she stood up but kept her feet hidden beneath the desk.

"Come up before the class," the teacher said. "I can't," Rachel replied. The teacher must have caught on that Rachel was ashamed of something, because she didn't say a word. When the final bell rang and all the children had left for the day, Rachel still sat on her feet. As the teacher prepared to leave, she simply said, "Rachel, I hope you feel better tomorrow." Rachel did. She went home and threw the shoes into the fire!

Children learn early to be ashamed if anything about themselves seems the least bit different from the norm. We aren't much more perceptive as adults. We value ourselves according to the clothes we wear, the house we live in, the kind of vacations we can afford. If they're not perfect, we downgrade ourselves. We have poor self-esteem.

Did you define yourself by describing your accomplishments or the kind of work you do? If so, you may be substituting the rewards that a career can bring for *self-love*. If you do well, you may develop self-confidence, and that is good. The danger is that without self-love you may be tempted to work harder and harder, trying to *earn* more love when God wants to *give* it to you without a price tag. You run the risk of becoming a kind of Scrooge, who tries to find happiness only in working hard and earning money. If you love yourself, you don't have to punish yourself by working harder all the time. You can give yourself permission to enjoy your family, friends, and other activities.

Did you write about your successes? If so, you may be confusing *self-confidence* with self-worth. Self-confidence is the force that enables you to get up and go. However, sometimes people keep on earning merit badges in order to overcome the feeling that they really *aren't* very worthy. The end result is that they become workaholics, or they spend so much time telling other people about their successes that everyone learns to avoid them. Inferior feelings don't go away until you realize that you are beautiful inside, no matter what you do or don't accomplish.

Did you attempt to define yourself by writing about your failures? If so, you are looking at your scars rather than at yourself. If you have achieved less than you would have liked, your *self-image* may suffer. Before Bob developed agoraphobia, he felt like a failure in his career, even though he had a successful executive search firm of his own at the age of thirty-three. He just couldn't forget that after college he had held six jobs in seven years. Besides, he told himself, his company should be making more money than it was. This poor self-image added to his stress. As a result, he developed agoraphobia.

Incidentally, while Bob had agoraphobia, he thought it was a terrible problem. Now he calls it a gift. Why? In order to recover, he was forced to learn how to see himself as a good person no matter how many times he failed. By changing his self-image, he became a person who could accept his worthiness. In turn, he was able to help countless others.

Worthiness 101

Now use the Second POWER Tool to obtain information that will help you feel beautiful on the inside. If there were such a thing as a college course in self-worth, it would have to begin with the fact that God loved each of us enough to make us in his image.

When we think about being made in God's image, we remember Jane's late Uncle Ed. Born prematurely, he was so tiny that Jane's grandparents laid him inside a fruit jar on barely warm ashes from the wood stove to keep him warm. He survived but was slightly mentally retarded. At age fourteen, he was still in the third grade despite his mother's having spent hour upon hour reading his lessons to him.

How could Ed be made in God's image? you might ask. Wasn't he, instead, some kind of reject? One day, the school bus driver decided to teach Ed to drive. Ed was thrilled. He learned so well that he was allowed to pick up the children and take them home in the evenings. Most exciting of all, he was allowed to keep the school bus at his house. Ed began to tinker with the diesel engine. He took it apart and put it together again. That was the beginning of a career for Ed. He became a diesel mechanic and worked for thirty-five years on road building equipment for Atlantic Bithulithic in Richmond, Virginia. Despite the fact that he could not read and write, he led a happy and productive life. Ed wasn't a reject, even though lots of people thought he was. Just like the East Texas land that the geologists considered of little value despite its vast pools of hidden oil, Ed had talents that no one had even suspected.

Today many companies recognize that most of their employees have barely tapped their hidden potential for productivity. They frequently ask Jane to speak to groups of their employees and help them develop a sense of self-worth. These companies recognize that people who feel beautiful from the inside out function better in their jobs.

"All of us have the same basic needs, yet each one of us is unique," Jane emphasizes. "God loves us for the uniqueness he has built into us."

You may be thinking, "That's just the trouble. No one else has a nose as big as mine. How can I feel beautiful inside when everyone's always looking at my nose?"

Perhaps your nose is really what's beautiful about you! Think of the pleasure Jimmy Durante and Bob Hope gave to so many by flaunting their famous noses.

If there were a college course in developing self-worth, it would continue with the fact that God loves us so much that he sent his son, Jesus, to demonstrate that love. Jesus talked about and practiced love in his short lifetime. He looked for the best in all humankind. As has been true of many individuals who espoused this revolutionary way of thinking about people, some wanted him dead. They captured him one day and, with all of the brutality you can imagine, they tortured him. They used a whip with a two-edged prong on the end of it to scourge him and tear his flesh. They pressed thorns into his skull, nailed his body to a cross, and allowed people to spit on him. When he was thirsty, they put bitter vinegar into his mouth. Jesus underwent all of that because he loved us enough to sacrifice his life and die. He wanted us to know that life holds more than what we see. He wanted us to know that we, too, can have this lovely Christ spirit within us.

Are we worthy? If we don't believe it, *we* are standing in the way.

What You Can Do to Feel Worthy

In his powerful book *Dynamic Imaging*, Norman Vincent Peale describes how he overcame a negative self-image and became a positive thinker who has inspired millions. He writes that his negative self-image stemmed from several childhood experiences. Being a "preacher's kid," he disliked being thrust into the limelight. Furthermore, he felt that he could never quite measure up to his unusually able, strong-minded, and outspoken parents. To make things worse, his physique was slender and lightweight, unlike that of his football-playing brother. By the time he went to college, he was so shy that he could not make a good showing in class. One day, as he tells it, Professor Ben Arnesson called him aside and demanded, "How long are you going to be like this—a scared rabbit afraid of the sound of your own voice? . . . You'd better change the way you think about yourself, Peale, and you'd better do it now, before it's too late."

Peale prayed that God would change him from a shy, insecure person to one who had the strength and confidence to do wonderful things. Peale believed that God would help him, and he did. Peale found that he could begin to speak up in class.

"The *image* I had had of myself was changed—and with it the course of my whole life," Peale says in the book. Peale learned after that that if he visualized himself as being the way he wanted to be while praying, he could become what he wanted. He also learned that he could change outside circumstances using the same methods.

Peale was using two of the techniques from the Third POWER Tool: positive prayer and visualization. If you are stuck because you don't feel beautiful from the inside out, working to master the Third POWER Tool's techniques will help you, too.

Consider the ways in which you have been trying to feel beautiful on the inside by associating your self-worth with others, your possessions, your career, or your successes or failures. Now write out ten affirmations about yourself. In doing this, ponder these questions:

1. Why are you a worthy person?
2. Do you become worthy through your own efforts or God's?
3. What are the qualities that you like about yourself?
4. What are the qualities you don't like about yourself?

Use your self-love to pat yourself on the back, and list the things that others tell you are good about yourself. Has anyone ever told you that you were a caring, loving person? Then love yourself enough to affirm that this quality is a wonderful way to be. Do others say you are a leader or a follower, an introvert or an extrovert? Whatever is said about you, affirm that it is good.

When you think about the qualities you don't like in yourself, reframe them into affirmations.

For instance, you might answer question 4 by saying, "I'm not a very assertive person," or "I'm not generous," or "I'm angry all the time." You can reframe these thoughts into affirmations by saying, "I *am* an assertive person," "I *am* generous and loving," and "I *am* calm and happy."

Write down *all* your affirmations—those that reflect how others tell you you are, and those that reflect how you want to be.

The next step is to *create visualizations based on the affirmations*. See yourself loving yourself enough to speak up to that grouchy boss or unthinking mate; see yourself being so generous that you are giving away mountains of dollar bills. Picture yourself floating on a placid lake, feeling completely calm and relaxed.

Finally, use these affirmations and visualizations as you pray. Ask God's help in bringing them about. Believe that God is changing you.

Actions Bring Change

By using the Fourth POWER Tool—engaging in risk-taking—you will train your mind to think differently about yourself. When Bob was practicing desensitization to recover from agoraphobia, he knew that he ran the risk of having a panic attack if he left his home. He did it anyway. He prepared himself by visualizing and affirming himself as being calm. He also knew that a panic attack wouldn't kill him. He learned to tell himself, "Yes, I feel panicky. My body is reacting to my sense of stress, but I'm really okay." After Bob risked going out many times, he had no more panic attacks. Feeling secure, he could leave home and do things that were fun. Risking helped him meet his goal of recovery from agoraphobia.

How can you risk feeling more beautiful inside? Take a small risk by exposing yourself to the very thing of which you are afraid! Visualizing and affirming ahead of time will reduce any discomfort you might feel. Risk believing that God has given you what you seek, even if it doesn't feel that way yet. When you have risked in a small way and succeeded, you will have enough confidence to take a bigger risk. Before you know it, you will have a wonderful feeling of self-worth.

For many people, shyness reinforces a feeling of unworthiness. Have you ever been at a meeting or a party where no one stepped forward to speak to you? When this happens, you have a choice. You can feel that something is terribly wrong with you, or you can risk putting out your hand and saying to the person next to you, "Hi, my name is _____. What's yours?"

If you take the risk, you will likely find that the other person will respond because you have shared names and touched each other. Your sense of worthiness will increase and your shyness will disappear.

If you take the further risk of making eye contact, the response will be even warmer. Jane explains at her human potential seminars that some people can't make eye contact because as a child someone angrily said to them, "Look me in the eye when I talk to you!" She advises those who have this difficulty to risk looking at the bridge of the nose of the person they are talking to, then sneaking a peek at his or her eyes every once in a while. When you begin to see the beauty found in the eyes, you will find you like to take this risk. You are connecting with the other person's soul.

At one seminar Jane attended, the audience experienced this beauty in an awesome way. Alan Cohen, who wrote *Rising in Love*, explained that an old Jewish legend holds that all the souls that were ever to be born were at one point together with God on Mount Sinai. Alan then asked everyone in the room to stand and greet each other as if they had once been together on Mount Sinai. Strangers hugged each other as if they were loved ones they hadn't seen in years. Somehow, it seemed true that they had once been together with God on Mount Sinai. Then, as Jane recalls it, Alan told them, "All our lives we listen to messages that say, 'You're not worthy because you're different. I won't speak to you.' When we tune out those messages, our natural being recognizes the life between us—not our personalities—but the light and life that is the Christ in us."

Another way to risk feeling beautiful is to accept compliments that others give you. What's the only appropriate response to a compliment? You're right: It's a simple "Thank you," even if you're thinking, "If you really knew me, you wouldn't say those things about me." Here is a fact: Those who share a compliment with you tell you the truth as they perceive you. They have no reason to lie. They could have left the words unsaid, but they took the risk of speaking lovingly to you. So take a risk yourself and believe that you are the way others tell you you are!

Many salespeople are functioning below par (and

consequently hurting their self-image) because they fear rejection. They find excuses for not making the calls they need to make and then tell themselves they're "just not very good at sales." If this is your problem, use the POWER tool techniques to make it easier; then take the risk of making those calls. Each little success will feed your self-confidence, which in turn will help you make future calls.

If you are afraid of criticism, risk doing things for which you will be judged. If you fear public speaking, make a point of doing it. Start out in a small way and progress to big things.

When Jane was a senior in high school, the Winston-Salem Jaycees asked her father if she would be their nominee in the Miss Winston-Salem pageant. Jane was horrified when she found that he had given them a tentative yes. How could she enter a beauty contest when a bathing suit would reveal her scars? At first she told her parents she wouldn't consider it.

Then her mother begged her to say yes. "Jane, if you can accept yourself and your beauty enough to risk the competition, then no matter how things turn out, you will be a winner," her mother said. Reluctantly, Jane agreed. She knew that she was a good dancer and that the contestants were scored 50 percent on their talents. Jane created a dance based on *Hamlet* that interpreted the pain Ophelia felt when Hamlet rejected her love for him. On the night of the talent judging, she felt as if she and Ophelia had become kindred spirits, as her body demonstrated the meaning of fear of rejection. The judges made her a finalist that night. Later she won the title of Miss Winston-Salem. She had risked exposing her scars, and they had been overlooked. Her mother had been right. Even if she hadn't won, her participation with the other talented young women and her creation of her dance would have been victories in themselves.

Right now, write down three small ways in which you will risk increasing your sense of worthiness. You might say, "Every time I think about my shortcomings, I will reframe them into affirmations." Or, "Whenever I am in a crowd and feel left out, I will risk introducing myself to someone." Or, "I will risk using visualizations and affirmations so that I can expose myself to the very thing I fear." You know what you want to change about yourself, so be specific in formulating your statements.

Now write out one *big* risk that you want to take in the future. You might write, "I want to risk becoming a manager in my office," or "I want to risk getting married," or "I want to risk getting my degree."

Developing a Habit of Love

The Fifth POWER Tool encourages you to reach out to others in order to reinforce gains, but you don't have to wait for gains to start using this tool. By helping others feel better about themselves, you will also gain a feeling of self-worth.

Every time Bob gives advice to a person who has a phobia, he feels good about himself. He knows that by helping another, he is making something good out of the bad things that happened to him. Reaching out makes him feel wonderful. Explaining how to conquer a phobia also reinforces these steps in his own mind.

You can start reaching out to others today simply by giving compliments to others. Find people who obviously don't feel good about themselves and look for one thing that they do well or that you find admirable. Then compliment them on that one thing. As Ken Blanchard explained in *The One Minute Manager*, such compliments can cause these persons to grow wonderfully. As you see the miracles you can work in others simply by sharing what you admire in them, your own self-confidence and self-esteem will increase as well.

Never underestimate the power of plain, simple love for others as a way of reaching out. When it becomes your second nature to accept others and love them for what they are, people will respond to you in ways that will make you feel beautiful inside.

Jane found a perfect example of this from a teacher she met in Hawkins, Texas. The teacher told of a former student who came to visit her in her classroom one summer just before school started. As she sat at her desk sorting materials for one more year of sophomore English, a nice-looking young man whom she didn't recognize came up and knelt down beside her. He began to thank her for being his teacher.

"I have a good job, a wonderful wife, and two little girls," he said proudly. As he showed her the photos in his billfold, she tried desperately to remember who he was, but she couldn't. She loved all her students, both the brainy ones and the not-so-smart ones, but there had been so many . . .

Then he said, "I came to tell you that I graduated from high school because of you. You see, I knew you loved me when I was your student because you would walk around the room while you lectured, and you would stop at my desk and put your hand on my shoulder."

The teacher knew this was her habit, but she hadn't realized it would seem important to anyone.

"When you returned my papers and they weren't very good, you always wrote something encouraging. But most important of all, when I was in your class, my daddy shot and killed my mother in a drunken argument. The other teachers acted as if they despised me, but you kept on treating me as if I were somebody. I want to thank you for loving me. It's made all the difference in my life."

The teacher hadn't even known that this tragedy had happened to him. She had simply loved *all* her students, without exception. Her *habit of love*—her touch, her encouraging words, her acceptance, and her general attitude of reaching out to others—had produced a miracle for this young man. What greater reward could she have for herself than his gratitude—and his success!

A Miracle for You

When God asked Moses to lead his people out of slavery in Egypt, Moses protested. Because he had murdered an Egyptian, he said, people didn't trust him. Besides, he was no leader. He couldn't even speak well in front of others.

Evidently Moses did not feel beautiful on the inside. He was stuck in feelings of unworthiness. When Moses at last believed that he had qualities that God wanted to use, he was able to risk asking Pharaoh to let God's people go. Moses became the greatest leader of the Old Testament.

We are created beautiful inside. We only have to believe it and risk acting as if we are that way. Then we will see miracles occur in our own lives, too.

6

Developing Your Sense of Humor —The Second Human Need

Rachel Carter, Jane's mother, once had an embarrassing moment that turned into a favorite humorous story for her family. While she was teaching in a model developmental reading school, her classroom had a two-way mirror along one wall so that visiting teachers could observe her techniques. Throughout the day, visitors came and went in the observation booth, but neither Rachel nor the children could see them.

One day, Rachel could hardly wait for the final bell to ring, because she was wearing a new girdle that had become unbearable. Once all the children were out of the classroom and on the bus, she took it for granted that the observation booth was empty. Standing in front of the big mirror, she pulled up her dress, yanked the instrument of torture off, and sighed with relief. Then she discovered that she had just taught the visitors one more lesson—one in immodesty. The twenty teachers who had been watching her final class had not left the booth, and they watched with fascination!

Rachel could have been so embarrassed that she never told anyone about this *faux pas*. Instead, she laughed at herself. She has told and retold this story through the years. Because she has a well-developed sense of humor, she doesn't mind sharing it with others, even though she is the butt of the joke.

Webster's Third International Dictionary defines humor as "that quality in a happening, an action, a situation or an expression of ideas which appeals to a sense of the ludicrous or absurdly incongruous elements . . . droll imagination or its expression." *We* define it as a basic human need.

Without humor you feel stuck in your depressions, worries, anxieties, and fears. Everything is deadly serious. The world is gray. Other people are an irritation, the future is hopeless, and you are helpless to do anything about it. What happens when you meet your need for humor? You laugh. Like magic, you feel better. The world has color in it. Other people seem friendly. God seems closer. You have hope that you can do something about the way the world is treating you. You are getting unstuck!

In his inspiring book *Tough Times Never Last, but Tough People Do*, Dr. Robert Schuller says, "You can't be a successful possibility thinker unless you can laugh at yourself and laugh at life's difficulties. If you keep your sense of humor and laugh, then you'll be able to love. I really don't think it's possible to love until you laugh first. People who try to love before they laugh take themselves too seriously."

We go one step farther and say that humor is a gift from God, a safety valve to release daily stresses, tensions, and anxieties. Laughter, as a friend of ours describes it, is "internal jogging." It keeps the spirit fit. When you are laughing, you can't be feeling the traumatic emotions that take their toll on your body, mind, and spirit.

How a Sense of Humor Can Help You Get Unstuck

How can an appreciation for the ludicrous or the absurdly incongruous be a tool with which you can dig yourself out of your rut? When you laugh, you learn better, make more friends, achieve better health, lessen the effects of trauma, even deepen your spiritual life.

While traveling by air recently, Jane watched a flight attendant brief passengers about safety procedures. Ordinarily passengers have heard this boring sing-song so many times that they don't bother to listen. This young man, however, caught their attention. "There may be fifty ways to leave your lover, but there are only seven exits on this airplane, so please look around and pick out the one you'd like to use if things don't go as planned," he said. Everyone laughed, but they did look around and find the nearest exit. Then he said, "Please put your seat back in its original upright and most *uncomfortable* position," and everyone did. When he ended with, "We certainly wouldn't want you to arrive at the terminal before the plane does, so please remain seated with your seat belt fastened," everyone applauded. These passengers listened to what he had to say because they hungered for humor. Any time you are stuck because you are having trouble learning, find ways to inject a little fun.

Folk wisdom holds that when you laugh you have lots of company. When you cry, you cry alone. You may be lucky to have one friend who listens patiently to your troubles, but you would probably have a lot more if you told a few jokes now and then. Even when you're not feeling happy, you can communicate better with your family and your coworkers if you deliberately seek to make them chuckle as well as sympathize.

Doctors who practice holistic medicine are now convinced of the truth of the old saying "Laughter is the best medicine." They recognize the body's ability to heal itself if the patient mobilizes mind, body, and spirit to oppose disease. Whenever you are feeling joy, your body is relaxed and operating normally. You breathe as you should, your heart beats at a restful pace, your muscles are unclenched. Your mind and spirit are exhilarated, too.

In his book *Anatomy of an Illness*, Norman Cousins credited laughter, vitamin C, and his will to live as the cure for his ankylosing spondylitis, a crippling disease that most doctors consider irreversible. He also discovered that ten minutes of belly laughter from watching old Marx Brothers films had an anesthetic effect that would give him at least two hours of pain-free sleep without pain medication.

Even if laughter doesn't heal your illness, it prevents you from being stuck in self-pity. A ninety-year-old woman whom Jane knew had become blind but remained remarkably cheerful. "How are you able to take your blindness so well?" Jane asked. "I remind myself that I had eighty-eight years of vision, and I'm grateful for that. Then I make it a point to laugh every day. If nothing happens that is funny, I just make it up," she said.

Humor can literally save your life when you are in the midst of traumatic situations, according to Gerald Coffee, a friend of ours who is a professional speaker. We have heard him tell how he survived seven years as a prisoner of war at the Hanoi Hilton by deliberately seeking out ways to experience humor. Even when he was shackled to his concrete slab of a bed, he could read the graffiti other prisoners had written on the wall. "Smile, you're on 'Candid Camera'" or "Guess who slept here" were statements ludicrous enough to help him keep his sanity.

If you are phobic, as Bob used to be, humor can break your paralyzing fear. Many phobics unconsciously hold their breath when they become anxious. They get on a plane, stop breathing, grip the armrests, and have a panic attack. Or they walk to a podium, forget to inhale, and find their voice choking up. When you laugh, you are forced to breathe from the abdomen. That is one reason why therapists often advise people who fear public speaking to begin speeches with a joke. The funny story not only creates smiling, receptive faces in the audience, it provides a break during which frightened speakers can inhale deeply. The fear-provoking adrenaline in their body stops flowing. Their shaky voice becomes steadier.

We're not saying that you should repress fear, anger, sadness, or depression. Sometimes it is best to acknowledge your emotions before you look for humor in a situation. Bob learned when he had agoraphobia that he could first tell himself, "Yes, I am feeling shaky, and that's okay," and then deliberately distract himself from his panic by looking for humorous things that others were doing. Unfortunately, many people are quick to acknowledge anger, disappointment, and resentment but slow to seek out humor. If you're feeling stuck, accept the emotions you are feeling and then quickly and deliberately move on, via humor.

Jane remembers a time when she felt badly stuck. We had been dating and discussing marriage when suddenly a disagreement caused us to break off our relationship. Jane felt depressed. She looked at her past and wondered why she had lost her marriage and several other important relationships. She realized that the needy little child inside of her was causing her to do a lot of things that prevented her from having a happy life. Ready to take therapy seriously, she chose Bioenergetics, which integrates the body, mind, and spirit.

The therapist first taught Jane to breathe properly. She was to avoid shallow breathing and to inhale all the way down in her abdomen. When she did, all the sadness she was feeling came pouring out. She found herself crying for no reason at all. The uncontrollable tears were a catharsis, her therapist told her. While the tears flowed, her diaphragm remained tight—a sign she had not let go completely of her stress and anxiety. Such tension could cause headaches, neck stiffness, back pain, stomach problems, and indigestion, so it was important to allow all the emotional pain to drain away.

One day during therapy, she felt that her diaphragm was on the point of relaxing. When her therapist pressed on it, she suddenly began to laugh.

"I had never experienced such glorious, blissful, happy laughter before. I felt a phenomenal glow. When I asked my therapist why I was laughing, he said, 'Don't talk, just laugh. The laughter is God.'"

Jane discovered that all the time she had been crying she had really been striving for the intense joy her therapist had called God. When she was able to let go of the sadness, the joyful God presence poured in. She felt renewed. Soon afterward, through what both of us consider a spiritual miracle, we were reunited and later married.

Theologian Reinhold Niebuhr wrote, "Humor is the prelude to faith and laughter the beginning of prayer." Recall the times when you have laughed so hard you couldn't stop. Weren't you more open to receiving all the good things God wanted to give you? Weren't you more willing to give of yourself to other people? Once your sense of humor has helped you develop a closer relationship with God, you will have the joy that Jane experienced.

We are convinced that by meeting your deep-seated need for a sense of humor, you can get unstuck. The question you may be asking now is "How do I do it?"

What's Your HQ?

Just as an Einstein with an IQ on the genius level finds it easier than most of us to understand how time and matter correlate, those fortunate people who are born with a sense of humor find it easier to laugh at themselves even when they make a mistake or things go wrong. If your "Humor Quotient" is low, however, don't beat yourself up about it. Just tell yourself, "I don't have a lot of laughter in my life; I don't have a lot of joy. I take things seriously, and I'd like to consider changing." Use the First POWER Tool to accept and love yourself enough to set goals to increase it.

Now, in your notebook, answer the questions below *true* or *false* to see exactly what your HQ is.

1. I enjoy hearing jokes told by others.
2. I usually tell one funny story or joke to at least one other person every day.
3. When I am sad or angry, jokes tend to raise my spirits.
4. A lot of things seem funny to me every day.
5. Whenever I feel blue, I look for the humorous things that happen around me to lift my spirits.
6. Whenever I've failed to accomplish things I wanted to do, I can find something to laugh about anyway.

7. I experience a good belly laugh every day.
8. I like to read the comics.
9. My family and friends say I have a good sense of humor.
10. Whenever I make a mistake, I accept the fact that I am human and try to find the amusing side of it.
11. I recognize that I deserve to take time to laugh.
12. I believe that laughter is a good thing.
13. Whenever I am sick, I seek out humorous TV programs to watch or amusing books to read.
14. Whenever I'm in a crowd, I note the amusing things that others do.
15. I take time to listen to the funny things that children say.
16. I have a lot of stories to tell about experiences that happened to me that didn't seem funny at the time but now do.
17. No matter how bad things seem, humor can help.
18. Whenever I'm in a group and I think of something funny to say, I go ahead and say it.
19. I'm not afraid to "let my little child out" to play and even act silly at times.
20. I don't mind risking saying something humorous whenever I'm with people who are all seriousness.

If you marked "true" on seventeen to twenty of these statements, you have already met your need for developing a sense of humor. With thirteen to sixteen marked true, you have a good sense of humor that will be an even greater asset if you develop it further. With nine to twelve marked true, you need to set goals to improve your sense of humor. If you marked fewer than nine true, you are probably feeling stuck. Developing a sense of humor will definitely help you get unstuck.

Now reframe all the statements you marked false as affirmations, and write them in your notebook. For instance, if you marked false the statement that you deserve to take time to laugh, reframe it as "I am a worthy person and I deserve to take time to laugh." Or, if you marked false the statement that you have a lot of funny stories to tell about things that happened to you that didn't seem funny at the time, reframe it as "I like to find the humor in everything that happens to me." Then think back. What are some of the most embarrassing things that have happened to you? What would seem funny about them if they had happened to someone else? Write some of these stories in your notebook. Resolve to share one of them with someone today.

Write why you think you are feeling stuck. Is there a way that humor could help you get unstuck? Write down five goals for injecting more humor into your life. For instance, you might write:

1. I will look for humor in situations that don't seem funny.
2. I will check out some humorous books from the library and read them.
3. I will memorize a joke and tell it to someone.

Obtaining Information to Help You Develop a Sense of Humor

It's not hard to use the Second POWER Tool to develop your sense of humor. Humorous books, movies, and TV shows abound. All you have to do is *decide* to visit a bookstore or library, select a movie, or flip on the TV. If you are not in the habit of doing such things, then set some goals to spend time every day exposing yourself to humorous things.

Don't forget to seek out the humorous things that happen in everyday life. Go to a playground and watch children giggle and laugh. Get on the merry-go-round or the see-saw with them. Listen to the funny things they say. Art Linkletter built a career by interviewing children on his long-standing "House Party" program and letting them say whatever they wanted. Their comments were sometimes uproarious. Why not "interview" a few of the children you know to receive your chuckles for the day?

A friend of Jane's, whom we'll call Miss Miller, was the epitome of the genteel and dignified Southern schoolteacher. She had taught first-graders for twenty-five years before the administration finally installed a student bathroom in her classroom. At first she was delighted. Then she found that at least one of her students didn't seem to know what the toilet was for. The floor around it was always wet!

"Children," she said in her soft voice, "Miss Miller has taught school for *so* long without a bathroom, and now she has one, and she is *so* proud of it. She wants to keep it clean and beautiful." Despite her understated pleas, the floor continued to be wet. Eventually Miss Miller resorted to a most unladylike strategy. She peeked and discovered the little boy who was the culprit.

"Son," she said gently, "Miss Miller wants so badly to keep her new bathroom nice and clean, but she can't if you wet on the floor. Now can't you help her?"

The little boy looked his teacher straight in the eye and said, "Miss Miller, have you ever tried to aim one of these things?" Even Miss Miller had a belly laugh out of that. Her frustration melted away.

Seeing Yourself as More Humorous

How rare is a sense of humor? When Jane co-headed her former company, Feedback, Plus, Inc., she stressed that one of the four secrets of quality customer service was a smile on the face of the person who meets the public. Whenever Jane sent secret shoppers out to businesses, she told them to check for smiles. Out of 200,000 secret shopping calls in 1987, only 3 percent of the individuals rated greeted the secret shopper with a smile. We believe that this is an indication that the majority of Americans lack a sense of humor.

"A customer being waited on really wants to see a smile. There's a light that comes with laughter. A smile that comes from deep down makes your face pretty," Jane says. "But the smile has to be genuine. If it's a faked smirk, it's worse than not smiling at all."

How deep-down is your smile? Look into the mirror and see whether it reflects a genuine feeling of happiness or whether it is forced. What can you do about it if you're stuck in so much gloom that you can't smile in a genuine way?

People in a rut can expose themselves to funny things twenty-four hours a day without feeling that they really have an inborn sense of humor. The Third POWER Tool will help you change your self-image from gloomy to joyous. Through positive prayer, visualizing, and affirming, you can let go of clenched teeth and frowns. You can enjoy humor and reflect it to others.

Jesus told his disciples, "Blessed are you who weep now, for you shall laugh." (Luke 6:22). God wants you to know joy. It is available if you accept it. If you are having trouble seeing anything funny in your life, ask God to give you his appreciation for the ludicrous and absurdly incongruous. Believe that he has already given it to you.

While you pray, use visualizations and affirmations. Remember a time when you laughed long and hard. See yourself in the setting where it happened. See the people who were with you. Spend a few moments enjoying the colors, the textures, the smells. Give thanks for this happy experience.

Now think of the situation that is making you feel stuck. Ask God to give you the same good feelings that laughter brought you *while you are picturing yourself in this situation*. See yourself wearing the same ear-to-ear smile while you participate in circumstances that cause you to feel stuck. Just as if you were an actor in a movie that has a happy ending, react to this experience with a smile or a joke. As you play this "film," repeat the affirmations you created after taking the Humor Quotient test. Remember that Jesus promised that you would laugh.

Such exercises may seem as if we are asking you to fake a sense of humor. You are exactly right! But if you spend ten minutes a day of your prayer time using these techniques, you will soon find yourself believing you *are* a person with a sense of humor. When you believe it, you can act on it.

The Adventure of Risking Humor

Like many people, we have an electronic telephone answering device. During the Christmas season, we decided that people who called didn't need the frustration of hearing an impersonal "I'm sorry I can't come to the phone right now." They were probably just as frantic as everyone else, trying to do their Christmas shopping and carry on their usual business. So we decided to inject a little humor. We taped a message in which each of us called out, "Merry Christmas!" Then Bob said, "We've gone Christmas shopping. We may even be buying a present for *you!*" And Jane said, "We hope you're buying one for us, too." Then we sang a verse of "We Wish You a Merry Christmas." Only then did we get down to business and ask the caller to leave a number so that we could return the call.

Corny? Perhaps. But what busy, frustrated person didn't have time to stop and smile when he or she heard it? Lots of callers told us they liked it. We risked letting our little child out and did something outrageous. We enjoyed the humor and so did everyone else.

Once you have learned to see yourself as a person who has a sense of humor, it's easy to use the Fourth POWER Tool to engage in the risk of doing something that is funny. You can start small by letting your own little child out. Go to the park; try skipping and laughing. Let yourself play!

Memorize a joke and tell it to your family. Then start telling jokes to other people. Find times when everyone else is deadly serious and risk telling your joke. As you discover how much fun this is, you may even learn to ad lib.

A bigger risk is to laugh at yourself when things go wrong. Even if you only make yourself the object of a ridiculous situation *to yourself*, it's a step forward. That is why we asked you to write in your notebook some of your most embarrassing moments. As you develop your sense of humor, you will find it is a positive experience to share these stories with others.

The great medical missionary Dr. Albert Schweitzer knew that life was not always easy for the three dozen or so European doctors and nurses who served in his hospital and leper colony in the equatorial African jungle. At dinner each evening, Dr. Schweitzer always had an amusing story to rejuvenate his staff members with laughter. Norman Cousins, who visited the Schweitzer hospital, reports in *Anatomy of an Illness* that one night the famous doctor told how he had been served Danish herring, a delicacy he didn't like, at the royal palace in Copenhagen. When no one was looking, he slipped the herring into his pocket. The next day a local newspaper reported that the doctor must have adopted primitive eating habits, for he had consumed the herring—bones, head, eyes, and all. The young doctors and nurses seemed as refreshed by this amusing personal story as by the food they were eating. "Humor at Lambarene was vital nourishment," concluded Cousins.

Reaching Out with Humor

Once you have developed your sense of humor, you will want to use the Fifth POWER Tool and reinforce it by reaching out to others. You have only to look around you at the many glum faces or listen to all the complaining or self-pitying voices to recognize how much the world *needs* you to spread humor. The wonderful thing about reaching out is that you not only help others; you also help yourself to retain your sense of humor each time you share it with others.

A friend of Pauline Neff's whom we'll call Ruth once visited a nursing home to cheer an elderly lady who was depressed over the loss of her loved ones and her health. As Ruth made pleasantries, the older woman leaned forward with a frown and complained, "Young lady, you may not know it, but your knees are exposed."

Ruth felt a bit miffed, because she knew her skirt wasn't too short. Still, she had come to help, not to cause problems, so she didn't react. She pulled her skirt down and kept smiling, even though the elderly lady's frown persisted. When at last Ruth stood up to leave, she patted her grouchy friend on the shoulder.

"Now, don't you tell anyone how many legs I have," she said. The older woman stared at Ruth for a moment and then started to laugh. She laughed so hard that tears came into her eyes. She looked twenty years younger!

Some of the experiences that happened to Bob when he had agoraphobia didn't seem funny at the time, but later he could laugh at them. He now reaches out to other agoraphobics with stories of how he once ordered a meal at a restaurant but then had to get up and leave before he could eat it. When he makes it seem funny, others who have panic attacks can laugh not only with Bob. They can laugh at the frightening things that happen to them.

A favorite story of Bob's is about the first time he gave a speech outside of the Toastmasters club. A chapter of the Lions Club had invited him to talk about his recovery from agoraphobia, and he wanted to look his professional best. That afternoon he went to his favorite barber, who kept a big jar of bubble gum for young customers. As was his habit, Bob let his little child out and treated himself to two big pieces of bubble gum.

Perhaps it was his nervousness over the coming speech, but while he was driving down the expressway, he mistook his tongue for the big wad of gum and bit down with gusto. Blood spurted out of his mouth. He had cut his tongue badly. It hurt, and it wouldn't stop bleeding. He raced home and put some ice on it. That helped alleviate the pain and stop the flow of blood, so he kept on munching ice. All during the Lions Club business meeting, he sucked on an ice cube. He talked as little as possible, because he didn't want to disturb his tongue.

When it came time to speak, Bob walked nervously to the podium. He began to speak, but the words coming out of his mouth sounded as if they were emerging from a package of marshmallows. His tongue had swollen and was so cold from the ice that his speech was almost unintelligible!

Bob could have let this embarrassing moment stop him from ever making another speech. Instead he found the humor in it. Now he uses this story as an example of how he risked making his first speech, failed miserably, forgave himself, and went on to become a professional speaker. It is also a way of using an experience that didn't seem so funny at the time as a way of reaching out with humor to others.

"To this day, I am sure the Lions Club has no idea of what agoraphobia is, but whatever they think it is, they know I hadn't recovered from it," he tells his audiences.

There are many ways to reach out to others with humor. Simply risk telling funny stories and jokes. Laugh at other people's jokes. Write someone a humorous note, or if you don't feel creative, send a funny greeting card.

It's Up to You

We're not the only ones who believe that you can start out sad, set goals to develop a sense of humor, then become so full of humor that you enliven others with it. In an interview in *Parade Magazine* (December 20, 1987), celebrated comedian Jonathan Winters reported how he grew up in an alcoholic home and later as an overworked star suffered a nervous breakdown. When a psychiatrist suggested shock treatment, Winters said, "I knew that in my complete package I carried around a great deal of pain—so maybe I should let them try to eliminate at least some of it. But I also knew that I carried around a good deal of knowledge, and what was going to happen to that? . . . Just what were they going to erase?"

Instead of losing those early and sometimes painful experiences, Winters opted not to have shock treatment. Instead, he gave priority to what was really important. He began to spend more time with his family and to paint as a hobby. He continues to make millions laugh by using his painful experiences in his impersonations of ordinary people.

"A lot of comedy stems from fear—and frustration," says Winters.

What can you do with your fears and frustrations? When your tire is stuck in the mud, you shovel sand into the rut to provide traction. By the same token, you can convert painful experiences into amusing stories that will help you move on once you have met your need to develop a sense of humor.

7

Getting Ship-Shape Physically —The Third Human Need

As a dancer herself, Jane was delighted to hear the famous New York choreographer Gabrielle Roth speak. Jane knew that Roth had created the dramatic modern dance "Pray Body." She was further impressed when she heard Roth tell the audience, "We are a celebration of life."

Jane agrees heartily. "In Gabrielle's dance, the beauty of the movements and the drama of the drumbeats evoke a feeling of awe that we have been given the wonderful gift of a body. We sense the need to honor and praise it," she says.

The Bible calls the body a holy temple, but many people forget that. They may adorn it with expensive fabrics and spend billions of dollars a year on cosmetics, jewels, and even fingernails, but they don't "pray body." Few of us treat our body like a holy temple.

Fully 20 percent of the U.S. population are overweight and some 53 million smoke despite the Surgeon General's warnings. Ten million are alcoholics, and during 1985 almost 23 million used illicit drugs, according to the National Household Survey on Alcoholism and Drug Abuse. Millions more abuse prescription drugs, and only a small percentage exercise properly. When we do not "pray body," we suffer from ulcers, migraines, low back pain, panic attacks, and high blood pressure. Worker absenteeism and medical bills go up. Productivity and harmony are disrupted.

A male child born today can expect to live to the age of seventy-one and a female to seventy-eight, simply because vaccinations have conquered diseases like smallpox, typhoid, cholera, measles, and diptheria. Antibiotics control many other illnesses. Americans today are succumbing to heart disease, hypertension, cancer, and diabetes—*chronic illnesses that relate to lifestyles.* Now, we ask you, what good is an additional quarter century of life if you can't enjoy it?

Consider this: You may be stuck in a poor relationship, a stymied career, family problems, or in depression and anger simply because you have not loved your body enough to keep it functioning as it should. When you're feeling bad, you don't have the energy you need to get out of these ruts. You can't even think clearly enough to know what to do!

Our Experience with Physical Fitness

When he was recovering from agoraphobia, Bob learned that he didn't just *have* a body. He *was* a body. When he didn't exercise, relax, or eat properly, and when he continued to drink coffee and alcohol, he was not giving his body the care it needed in order to deal with stress. Accordingly, his body sent him panic attacks that kept him stuck at home for months.

In order to become physically fit, Bob first went to

the doctor for a checkup. He discovered that he was twenty-seven pounds overweight and that his cholesterol and triglyceride levels were too high. Because his father had died of a heart attack and his mother had also had one, he made goals to normalize his blood chemistry and lose weight. Then he studied books on nutrition in order to devise his own "Sensible Eating Plan." By using some of the same tools that we advocate in this book (visualizing, affirming, and risking) he lost twenty-seven pounds, worked up to jogging in ten-kilometer races, and reduced his cholesterol and triglyceride levels to normal.

Simultaneously, Bob stopped putting substances in his body that increased his anxiety. For him that meant no more caffeine, excess sugar, and alcohol. (He had given up cigarettes long before.) Though he did not have a drinking problem, he was surprised at how much the quality of his life improved when he didn't numb his senses with excess food and drink. He could go to a party and have just as much fun as anyone else without worrying about having to drive while under the influence or facing a hangover the next morning.

When Bob had achieved all his physical fitness goals, his panic attacks were gone for good. He felt wonderful! Soon afterward, he found Life Plus.

Being a dancer, Jane has always had a healthy respect for physical fitness. Nonetheless, in her late twenties she didn't do anything to keep herself in top shape. On the day she turned thirty, the physical education teacher at the school where she taught told her he had just read Dr. Kenneth Cooper's book *Aerobics*. He wanted all the teachers to put a couple of dollars in a kitty, which would be awarded to the one who could earn the most points for aerobic exercise by the end of the school year.

"He asked me what I did for physical fitness. I had to admit that all I did was chase after a nine-year-old. Dr. Cooper didn't award any points for that! But I really wanted to win the contest, so the next day I put on my shorts and went out to the school track. Then I realized I was ashamed of the way my legs looked. That was enough motivation to get me started exercising," says Jane.

"After I began running, I changed my eating habits. I cut down on red meat, because I couldn't run and digest it well. I soon went from a size nine to a size four. I ran several ten-kilometer races, and I even began to teach aerobic dance classes. I had never looked or felt so good in my life! I finally knew how wonderful it felt to live in a fit body."

Both of us have slipped several times in our desire to keep on being physically fit. When we stopped exercising and eating right, we gained weight and felt fatigued. Little aches and pains returned, and our mental sharpness diminished. Then, each time we started exercising again, we felt so good that we asked ourselves, "Why do we *not* do this? It's great to feel the wind blowing on our skin. It's so enjoyable to breathe deeply and feel our bodies sweat and function as they should."

When Jane moved to Texas, she was not only stuck mentally but stopped exercising and eating right.

"I gave myself a thousand excuses. It was too hot to run. I didn't know the neighborhood. I might miss a phone call from North Carolina. I tried to fill up the emptiness in my life by giving myself permission to eat a lot of steak and potatoes.

"Then, after my divorce, when I was *really* down, I got into the trap of drinking more than I should. It became a social thing as a single to have a glass of wine or meet for happy hour or have a cocktail. I kept alcohol in the house for friends who might drop by. The next thing I knew, I was having a drink by myself every time I felt a little bit down. When I felt up, I would have a little drink so that I could sleep. I was never an alcoholic, but after I stopped drinking, I realized how overly sensitive and irritable alcohol had made me."

Both of us drank socially while we were single. One Valentine's Day when we were dating, we had several glasses of wine before and during our meal. Afterward we got into a terrible argument over a difference we now consider no bigger than a molehill. The next day we talked it over and realized that we just could not communicate effectively when our minds were altered by alcohol. We decided in that moment to give it up entirely, and we've never been sorry. We just don't drink any more. Our sobriety hasn't interfered with our social life at all. We find, too, that a lot of other people are relieved that they don't have to drink to keep us company. In business, clients are happier to see us completely sober. They know we've got our minds on the job.

We're not fanatics about any of these lifestyle changes. When we slip up, we don't beat ourselves over the head about it. In fact, we often apply what we call "the 75 percent rule." If we're doing all we should do to be physically fit 75 percent of the time, that's good. When we're not, we remind ourselves that we are still worthy human beings. Then we start over on our goals.

By meeting our need to feel physically fit, we increase our chances of not getting stuck no matter what happens to us.

Who's Responsible, Anyway?

You are responsible for the condition your body is in right now. If you are ship-shape, congratulate yourself for doing a good job. But don't become complacent! Your body can put up with a lot before it sends you a major catastrophe. One way to tell whether you are being kind to your body or not is to ask yourself the questions that follow:

Do you often feel that you just don't want to be with other people because you don't look good in your clothes? Do you feel tired all the time? Your eating habits may cause you to weigh too much or too little. Your nutrition may be so poor that you lack energy. If so, take responsibility for your situation and then use the Second POWER Tool to obtain the information you need to eat right. (We'll give you tips for how to do this later in this chapter.)

Do you have trouble sleeping? Is it an effort to bend over and pick up a coin you dropped? Do you frequently have a pounding heart, sweaty palms, or a dry mouth—symptoms of anxiety that your doctor says have no physical cause? If so, you may not be giving your body the exercise it needs. You can change that by setting up daily exercise routines—starting off slowly and working your way to a new level of fitness.

Do you smoke? If so, you already know you are reducing your lung capacity and risking cancer. Even if you have tried unsuccessfully to stop smoking, you *can* quit by using the POWER tools.

How many cups of coffee, glasses of tea, or cans of cola do you drink every day? You may think that these caffeine-containing drinks "pick you up" and make you feel good. Doctors will tell you that after their effect has worn off, you feel more tired than if you had never drunk them. You can make a resolution to keep anxiety-producing caffeine out of your system.

When something bad happens, do you reach for a drink or a tranquilizer? Is a party not a party to you unless the punch is alcoholic or someone hands you a joint? Is alcohol, cocaine, or any other mind-altering drug causing problems with your family, your career, or compliance with the law? Even if you are using a mind-changing chemical recreationally and are not addicted to it, you are short-changing your body. Only you can make the decision to quit.

Don't wait for a major crisis to decide that you are going to change these habits. Jane took her physical well-being for granted until her doctor told her she had an ovary that was hardened and enlarged and needed to be removed. She was so fearful that the cancer she had had as a child was returning that she reacted irrationally. She refused the surgery and told her husband and parents nothing. After two months of being stuck in frantic fear, she came home after trick-or-treating with her son on Halloween and found her doctor waiting with her family. Together they insisted that she have the surgery. She did—the next day. There was no sign of malignancy.

"I had thought that cancer was going to cause me to lose everything I cared about—my relationship to my son, my career, my life. Once the surgery revealed that I was okay, I never wanted to risk losing those things again. Within a month I was walking a mile. Within two months I was running a mile and signing up for a university class to learn the choreography for ten major musicals in twenty weeks! I danced every day," Jane remembers.

Count Your Body's Blessings

Do you appreciate the blessings that a fit body automatically gives you? Count a few:

- More energy—to work or play as hard as you want and to enjoy it more
- Mental sharpness—to understand faster and to be more creative on the job
- Better sexual performance—to celebrate intimacy with the one you love
- An increased attention span—to be more productive in your work and reap the financial rewards
- Improved relationships—to feel like solving conflicts and accepting other people
- More strength—to create with your hands, to garden, or to excel in sports
- Improved appearance—to enjoy being you
- A better self-image—to enable you to use your talents and reach out to others

We could go on and on about how wonderful it is to feel and look great because you're healthy. Think of the last time you felt miserable with a cold or the flu. You know that a healthy, beautiful body is a blessing. Why not honor it by *keeping* it fit?

Tips for Making Exercise Enjoyable

If your spirit is willing to start exercising but your body is not, see yourself as you really are. Ask yourself how many minutes a day you spend in exercising. Compare yourself with the standards that experts like Dr. Kenneth Cooper uphold in *Aerobics*. Then ask yourself,

"Would I be willing to recommend my present lifestyle to my children?" If you can't, then be your own best friend and set long-term goals for change. Break these goals down into such small increments that they don't seem insurmountable.

If you find an activity that is enjoyable to you, it will be easier to exercise. Both of us enjoy jogging, but you might prefer riding a bicycle, swimming, jumping rope, playing aerial tennis, or working out on Nautilus equipment. Whenever you can, do your exercising with other people. Make a social event out of it. By competing with them and encouraging them, you will be reinforcing your own desire to keep on keeping on.

Think of the benefits you will achieve. Jane's father, Miles Carter, proved that you not only feel better when you are fit, but your productivity is improved and you are better able to relate to other people. Back in the 1950's, he set up one of the first corporate recreation programs in the nation for the McLean Trucking Company. Both union and nonunion workers participated side by side in baseball, golf, swimming, bowling, fishing, even square dancing and bridge. His theory was that people who play together get along better. McLean's labor relations were superb. Because a vice-president played baseball with a dock man or warehouseman, they could communicate better. Miles Carter received the coveted Helms Award for excellence in recreation, and now many corporations have such programs.

Using the POWER Tools to "Pray Body"

If you are feeling fat, flabby, or frustrated because you eat the wrong things or drink or smoke, *don't* berate yourself with guilt-producing statements. Using the First

POWER Tool to accept yourself as you are enables you to acknowledge:

- That you have a problem
- That, even so, you are a worthy human being, a child of God, who deserves to be physically fit, enjoy life, and have energy and enthusiasm

You can substitute health-producing routines for bad habits by writing out some short- and long-term goals. When you start working on them, you will find that the routines become enjoyable in themselves. That is exactly what Bob did when he discovered that he could reduce his anxiety through exercising and better nutrition. First he set long-term goals to lose twenty-seven pounds and to be able to jog fifteen miles a week. He knew that he couldn't reach these goals in a single day, however, so he set daily short-term goals that would be relatively easy to achieve. For the exercise goal, for instance, he started out walking two miles a day, walking a little faster each day. Each week he set new short-term goals that stretched his endurance a little further. By the end of three months, he had a short-term goal to jog three miles at a time.

Here is how his first week's short-term goals looked.

Jogging:
1. Read a book on how to begin doing aerobic exercises safely.
2. Learn how to monitor my heart rate.
3. Walk two miles a little faster each day until I can walk two miles within thirty-four minutes.

Losing weight:
1. Read a book on nutrition and weight control.

2. Create menus based on 1200 calories per day and a balanced diet.

3. Start following the new menus.

4. Make a chart to record my daily weight gain or loss.

"Physical fitness goals always seem monstrously large," Bob says. "That's why it's important to work on them one day at a time. *Today* we don't have a drink or a cigarette. *Today* we only have to lose a few ounces of weight. Set a firm goal. Then break it down into small parts, and reward yourself for accomplishing both the big and little goals.

Jane knew a man who carried the same pack of cigarettes in his pocket for twenty years without smoking. He needed the security of knowing the cigarettes were there if he felt compelled to smoke. He also could tell himself, "I believe I'll put off smoking until after breakfast." Then it was "after going to work," "after coffee break," or "after lunch." By putting off smoking, he got through twenty years, one day at a time.

Obtaining information relevant to your needs is not hard when bookstores and libraries have entire sections on nutrition, exercise, and addictions. Another source is your doctor. Before you start working on physical fitness goals, you must have a physical examination to tell you how much you can exercise safely. You can also pinpoint problems with cholesterol, triglycerides, blood pressure, or other limitations. Additional sources of information may be available through government publications and support groups. Check the library and Yellow Pages to locate them. Make this one of your goals.

Working to master the techniques means using positive prayer. Jesus said that just as a father knows how to

give good gifts to his children, "how much more will
your Father who is in heaven give good things to those
who ask him!" (Matthew 7:11). If you ask God to help
you keep your body in the optimum condition in which
he gave it to you, he will do so, *if you do your part by
living a fit lifestyle*. Visualize yourself eating nutritious
foods and liking them, or exercising with a smile on
your face. See yourself with the body you want on the
beach, at a party, or with the person you love. Affirm,
"I like to jog, or swim, or eat sensibly, or live without
cigarettes." You will find to your surprise that you do
begin to enjoy fitness routines. You will find yourself
achieving goals with much less effort than you thought
possible.

Don't Be Deceived by Setbacks

Engaging in risk-taking means actually getting out of
the house and taking the first step on your two-mile
walk before you go to work, or putting off that drink
you'd like to have. It also means that you risk failing.
That's okay. Through lots of personal experience with
fitness goals, we know that setbacks are going to happen. When they do, *we don't give up*. We simply pick
ourselves up and keep going.

"When I first began to exercise, I set goals to run
every day," Bob says. "Then a cold spell would come
or I'd feel sore, so I would lay off for a week or so. I
told myself I was nothing better than a yo-yo, because
I had promised myself I would achieve the goal I had
set. I had to learn that when you venture into new
territory, you're going to hit some bumps on the road,
but that's okay."

Jane made the opposite mistake when she entered
the fitness contest at her school. She tried to do too

much all at once. "The very first day I went out to the track and ran a mile. The next day I was so sore I could hardly move! Someone told me that what I needed to do was to run some more, so the second day I ran another mile. By the third day I was so stiff that I had to crawl out of bed and soak in the tub before I could go to school. Now I know that that is not the way to start exercising. Reputable fitness books tell you to start out slowly and gradually increase the amount you exercise so that your body can easily adjust to the new routines."

Go Public with Your Commitment

How can you motivate yourself to keep on working on fitness goals?

- Don't wait for others to notice that you are committed to becoming fit. Tell everyone who will listen about your plans. Others will shower you with encouragement and information. Their congratulations for achieving a short-term goal will help make it easier for you to put out a little more effort the next day.
- Subscribe to a fitness magazine and learn ways to make exercising easier and more fun.
- Go to a sporting goods store and get excited by all the great equipment you can learn to use.
- Create an incentive program. Buy yourself a new workout suit . . . funny shoelaces for your sneakers . . . a Walkman for achieving a short-term goal.
- Use the Fifth POWER Tool and *reach out to reinforce* your gains. When others note that you've given up smoking or started eating a different diet, tell them how much better you feel. Pass on the information you've obtained about physical fitness and encourage

them to begin to feel as great as you do.

- Better yet, get yourself a partner. Then both of you can reach out to encourage each other to stay on your new routines. Or join a support group and reach out by patting others on the back for their progress. Each time you help someone else, you are reinforcing your desire and ability to succeed at a fitness routine.

One of the best ways to reach out is to use this marvelous body you have as it was meant to be used. "Our bodies were designed to sweat, work, breathe, and to be enjoyed," Bob likes to say.

Tips for Eating the Right Stuff

Like most people, Bob became concerned about his diet when he realized that he was twenty-seven pounds overweight. He thought that if he ate fewer calories, his body would be lean and fit. When he began obtaining accurate information, however, he realized that counting calories wasn't enough. In order to keep off the weight and become truly healthy, he needed to consider the nutritional value of the food he was consuming, and he needed to exercise. Like most Americans, he wasn't eating nearly enough vegetables and grains. Instead, he was loading up on meat, which has a high content of saturated fats that only increase one's cholesterol level. At first, his solution was to start opening cans of vegetables. Not until later did he realize that vegetables have the highest nutritional value when they are eaten fresh—raw or lightly steamed.

After reading many books and magazine articles on nutrition, Bob devised his own "Sensible Eating Plan." It included foods from all four of the basic food groups recommended by the U.S. Department of Agriculture's

Daily Food Plan—dairy, meat, vegetables and fruits, and grains. Because his cholesterol level was high, he ate less meat and more complex carbohydrates. He eliminated sugar and held his daily calorie level to 1200 while he was losing weight and to 1500 later in order to maintain his proper weight.

At the same time, Bob visualized himself as being thinner and more fit. He affirmed that he enjoyed eating sensibly. He was surprised to find that he was able to hold to his new plan. He wasn't so fanatic that he couldn't enjoy an occasional meal out with friends, but he did hold to it at least 75 percent of the time.

To devise your own Sensible Eating Plan, consider the physical challenges you have. Do you need to lose weight? Gain weight? Feel more energetic? Overcome cholesterol problems? If so, study nutrition and devise your own plan accordingly. Then use positive prayer, visualizing, and affirming to motivate you to risk changing your behavior.

Tips for Giving Up Smoking

Jane's friend never believed she could stop smoking until the day she went for a facial. The cosmetologist took one look at her skin and told her, "I see you are a smoker. Smokers always start having wrinkles earlier than nonsmokers." Her friend threw away her cigarettes that day and never had another.

If such a traumatic event has not occurred in your life, you may believe that you "just can't quit." Just as you can give up any other bad habit by replacing it with something better, you can stop smoking. You need to find a new activity that is more enjoyable and substitute it for the pleasure you get from cigarettes. We know lots of people who give up smoking when they start running, because they can't run as fast or as far as they want if their breathing is limited by smoking. Once they have given up cigarettes, they receive an additional pay-off: They know they have conquered a bad habit. They are a success! They are overcomers!

Think about why you smoke. Is it a social activity that you enjoy doing with others? Do you believe that it keeps you from being nervous? Is it an after-meal plus? Are you afraid you'll substitute food and gain weight? Write in your notebook the reasons for your smoking. Then counter them with affirmations such as "I can enjoy the company of others more without a cigarette," or "I am perfectly calm without smoking," or "My food tastes better if I'm not smoking," or "I can substitute jogging for smoking and enjoy life more." Use these affirmations to construct visualizations of yourself. Then use positive prayer to ask God's help.

Once you have prepared yourself mentally, obtain information that will help you set your goals. You may be the type who can quit "cold turkey," as Bob did, or you may prefer to reduce the amount you smoke gradually. You may want to enroll in a special program designed to help you quit smoking, or join a support group. Find a partner—someone who also is quitting smoking or has already stopped. Reach out, and let others reach out to you.

Write out your goals, both long-term and short-term. If you are gradually cutting back, keep records in your notebook of how much you are smoking and affirm your progress frequently. For instance, you might write in your notebook:

"I did really well today because I cut back by six cigarettes."

"I had two cigarettes today, but that's a lot better

than in the past. Tomorrow I have another chance to be smoke-free."

"Today when I felt I had to smoke I called a friend and talked until I overcame the craving."

Tips for Giving Up Substance Abuse

Accepting yourself as you are is crucial to giving up mind-altering chemicals. Is your "search for the spirits" one that you can handle, or is it a problem that requires professional help? Unfortunately, if you are actually addicted, you will probably deny it, because these substances confuse thinking processes. If you're not sure whether you are abusing drugs, try doing without alcohol, a tranquilizer, or any other psychotropic chemical for a month. If you can do it without having any physical or emotional signs of withdrawal, you probably don't have a serious problem with it.

To assess this, ask yourself the following questions:

1. Do I experience a meaningful change from the use of alcohol or drugs? Do I depend on alcohol or medications to relieve tension, fears, anxieties, or inhibitions?

2. Do I find myself involved increasingly in thoughts about alcohol or drugs? Am I thinking about whether I have enough of these substances when I could be thinking of other things?

3. Do I prefer drinking or taking drugs to associating with family and friends?

4. Do I prefer drinking or using drugs to hobbies I formerly had?

5. Has my drinking and/or use of drugs become more secretive, more guarded?

6. Am I drinking more and more heavily than in the past?

7. Do I ask for medications for pain, anxiety, or sleeping disturbances from more than one doctor, without informing each physician about the other prescriptions? Do I continue drinking even when I know that alcohol should not be combined with a medication I am taking?

8. Do I tell myself I am handling my problem because I maintain periods of not drinking or using drugs in between binges?

9. Am I kidding myself that by drinking beer or wine instead of Scotch or by smoking marijuana rather than taking cocaine that I am cutting down?

10. When I start drinking alcohol or using drugs, do I end up taking more than I intended?

11. Have I failed to remember what occurred during a period of drinking or using drugs at any time?

12. Do I find it hard to concentrate, pay attention in class, or remember things that happened just a few moments ago?

13. Do I feel guilty, defensive, or angry when someone wants to talk to me about my drinking or use of drugs?

14. Am I sneaking my drinks and/or pills?

15. Have I stopped sipping my drinks and instead find myself gulping or tossing them down quickly? Do I

take more of a prescribed drug than the doctor ordered?

16. Do I lie about my drinking or use of drugs?

If after answering these questions you feel that you have a problem, *do not fail* to get professional help. It is impossible to overcome physical or psychological addiction by yourself. You can get the addresses of qualified counselors and support groups from your county or state council on alcoholism and drug abuse. Millions have succeeded in this way, so don't be discouraged. Their joyful stories of recovery are an inspiration.

If, on the other hand, your problem is not severe, you might do as Jane did and replace the rituals of drinking with pleasant nonalcoholic ones. For instance, she usually came home from work, poured herself a glass of wine, and put her feet up to relax. The only thing she changed about that ritual was to substitute a glass of sparkling water for the wine. You can do the same. Sip a glass of fruit juice rather than a can of beer while you're watching TV. When entertaining friends, drink orange juice mixed with bubbly ginger ale rather than a cocktail.

These substitutions worked for Jane, but even so, it wasn't easy. "I hadn't considered myself an alcoholic because I never got drunk or caused a scene. But I couldn't believe how much I wanted a drink until I tried to stop."

Positive prayer with visualizations and affirmations helped her overcome the craving. For instance, when preparing to go to a social event, she would visualize herself at the party, laughing and talking with her favorite people. She would hear her friends telling her that she looked great, and she would see herself reaching out to others with love. She would repeat affirmations that she had previously written in her notebook, such as "'God richly furnishes us with everything to enjoy' (I Timothy 6:17), so I feel relaxed and confident that he will provide me with happiness at the party without alcohol."

When she was feeling lonely or depressed, she asked God to help her relax without the use of alcohol. She visualized herself enjoying an evening of solitude reading a wonderful book, watching a favorite TV program, or luxuriating in a hot bath. She used such affirmations as "I can enjoy being alone," or "Because I was made in God's image, I can be perfectly happy without alcohol." Then she would thank God for being with her and bringing the "peace that passes all understanding" (Philippians 4:7)

Where to Start

If meeting this need seems overwhelming, remember that you don't have to do it all in one day. Just make a start by choosing the *one change* that is *most important* to you. Once you begin, you will feel so much better that you will want to go on and make further improvements.

As chairperson of the Health and Fitness Special Interest Group of the National Speakers Association, Bob has planned aerobics events for the association's annual convention. We think it's impressive to see nationally recognized speakers like Zig Ziglar and Ed Foreman run several miles and then give energy-charged speeches that motivate everyone to become a success. Lots of professional speakers sip juice and munch on apples rather than coffee and doughnuts during "energy breaks." They are only practicing what they preach—

that you have to be sound mentally, spiritually, *and physically* to live life at the 100 percent level. If you are stuck in any kind of situation, meeting your need to "pray body" will go a long way toward getting you unstuck.

8

Getting Out of the Prison
of Your Thoughts
—The Fourth Human Need

Before Bob overcame agoraphobia, Mr. Negative used to call him many times a day, telling him, "You're a failure. You should be able to leave the house like other people, but you can't. You're going to lose your business." Every time the phone rang, Bob picked it up and listened to Mr. Negative on the line. Afterward he felt worse than ever. Anxiety and depression were his constant companions. It was as if his thoughts had constructed a prison around him and he couldn't get out.

"Whatever you think about intently creates that reality in your own life," Bob says. "If you worry, if you constantly predict dire circumstances, if you are always saying 'ain't it awful,' you are inviting the things you *don't* want to happen to materialize. On the other hand, if you dream great dreams and expect wonderful things to happen to you, you open the way for these things to occur."

When Bob learned to stop answering the phone each

time Mr. Negative called, and when he replaced fearful thoughts with affirmations, the prison walls tumbled down. He was freed of the awful panic attacks. Not only that, but when he focused on positive things, he could see that the world was a rainbow of color rather than black and white. Eventually Mr. Negative, tired of not having his calls answered, stopped dialing Bob's number.

One day when Bob was on a radio show urging listeners to affirm the good things in their lives, a woman with a weary voice called in to complain, "Don't you think you're looking at the world through rose-colored glasses?" She went on to tell him that she never slept more than two hours every night. She lay in bed flooded with reminders of all the bad things that had happened to her and all the worse things she was certain would happen. She felt terrible. "You just can't start thinking positive thoughts if you don't feel like it," she said.

This woman was trapped in a vicious circle. Her negative thoughts were creating bad feelings, which in turn caused her to think more negative thoughts, which made her feel worse.

"If you want to feel good, you must first *think* positively. Then the good feelings will come," Bob told her. "Fake it at first, if you have to. Eventually you will develop the habit of thinking positively."

The woman didn't sound convinced. She was stuck in the prison of her thoughts, convinced that she was a loser, the victim of hard luck. The door to the exciting and beautiful world outside wasn't going to open for her until she risked making changes in her thinking.

Jane sees many people like this woman in her seminars. "Whatever comes, they just take it. They get up in the morning, go to work, spend all their effort trying to dodge other people who get in their way, go home, drink their beer, and go to bed. The next morning they wake up and say, 'What's it all about? My life doesn't mean anything.' It really doesn't, because they are *re-acting* rather than *acting*. They are just living, if you can call it that, until they die," she says.

They have excuses, of course. They've broken up with a boyfriend, lost their job, become discouraged over a problem with their children, found a gray hair, lost money on the stock market, and on and on. They listen to Mr. Negative telling them they are a failure. They chew on these thoughts, digest them, and create additional "hard luck" for themselves.

If you feel this way, you haven't fulfilled your need to develop a positive mental attitude. Seeing only hardships in your life, you will feel too burdened to get out of your rut.

The "Is It Bad or Is It Good?" Game

In our office is an abstract painting. Some people look at it and see a beautiful young woman. Others see an old woman, yet it is the same picture. How does this happen? Are people born with an optimistic viewpoint? And if they are not, can they cultivate one? We are sure that they can.

Long ago, a king owned a beautiful stallion that was the pride and joy of his son, a handsome young prince. One day the stallion ran away and could not be found. Was that bad or good? If you think it's bad, consider the fact that several months later the stallion returned, bringing with him one hundred wild horses just as beautiful as himself. Was that bad or good? Good, you might say. But the next day when the prince tried to break one of the wild horses, he was thrown. His leg was horribly broken. Was that bad or good? Bad? The following week a war was declared. All able-bodied men were conscripted for service in the army. Most were killed in a bloody battle. The king's son didn't have to go to war, however, because of his broken leg. So it was good.

By now you get the point. Whether something is bad or good depends on the way you see it. Ask yourself why a home in Beverly Hills or Hyde Park is worth more than if that same home were in a middle-class neighborhood. Isn't it that you see it differently? Your *perception* of its worth adds to its value.

How do you see yourself? Are you a person of great worth? Do you deserve good or bad things? If you perceive yourself as created in the image of God, you will know that regardless of how you see your successes or failures, you are precious in his sight. In fact, Genesis says that God thinks so highly of you that he has given you dominion of the world. He has made you in such a way that you are capable of taking care of it for him. If you are thinking negatively and saying, "I can't make changes in my life because of my husband, or my boss, or the bills, or my illness," or, "No matter what I do, I feel like a loser," you are looking at a good thing and calling it bad. *You* are the one who is preventing yourself from taking dominion and enjoying the gifts of the world.

What Color Glasses Are You Wearing?

Are you feeling happiness, joy, success, contentment? If not, have you ever stopped to ask yourself where these feelings come from? Why do other people succeed in love, careers, and relationships while you feel that you lag behind? Could it be the result of choosing smoked glasses rather than rose-colored ones?

Think about something that has happened to you recently that you consider bad. Write in your notebook the feelings you have about it. Are you angry? Bitter? Envious? Frustrated? Now think where these feelings come from. Are they the result of the thoughts or perceptions you have about this event? Do you believe that this event has cost you love, money, power, friendship, prestige, or anything else?

Now consider whether you, like the king's son, have in the long run gained anything through this event. If you are in the habit of thinking negatively, you may have to look hard. Have you grown spiritually? Are you better able to identify with others who have gone through similar circumstances? Do you appreciate things more? If so, write down the ways you have grown. Write down any other good result. This is how to perceive events in a positive way. It is also a good technique for changing your feelings and opening yourself to the wonderful gifts available to you.

Now think about some worry that you have about the future. Why are you feeling fear? Does this feeling come from your thoughts? If so, what are your thoughts? Do you believe you will suffer a loss of some kind?

In your notebook, write down the way you would like the future to turn out. Be extravagant! See yourself gaining rather than losing. This is the positive way to look at the future. You will be rewarded with good things if you think this way.

Beth, a young businesswoman, told Jane, "I was really unhappy in my work because everyone else seemed to avoid me. I was so lonely and felt so rejected that I couldn't concentrate. One day my boss called me into her office and told me that I had a bad attitude.

'Me?' I said. 'Other people are the ones who have the bad attitude. They never invite me to go to lunch with them. They never make small talk with me. They just want to get out of my office as fast as they can.' Then my boss said, 'Could it be that it's because you never say good morning to anyone? Or that you always close the door to your office rather than leaving it open?' I realized that what she said was true. I was *feeling* alienated and so I was *acting* in ways that caused the alienation to increase."

But where did the feelings come from? Beth's poor self-image made her believe that she was not attractive to other people. In the long run, *this negative thought created the very reality she most feared*. Beth used the First POWER Tool to see herself as the worthy person she really was. She wrote down the thought "People don't like me," and countered it with the affirmation "I am a likeable person because I was created in the image of God." She also wrote down the good things about her embarrassing interview with her boss: She had received feedback that was going to help her. By choosing to think positively rather than negatively, Beth was able to risk more outgoing behavior. She started to leave her office door open and say good morning to everyone. Soon she began developing friendships with the other workers.

You can see things as sad or happy, awful or excellent, dull or exciting. You have the choice. You can see a problem and call it a challenge. You can see a worry and call it an opportunity. Don't worry if you are faking at first. Your feelings—and your opportunities—will change for the better if your thoughts do.

Changing Your Perception of Yourself

As a teacher, Jane was once assigned the dubious task of teaching twelve illiterate fifteen-year-old boys how to read. Because they were all troublemakers, their classroom was a trailer set far away from the school building. When they swaggered into the makeshift class-room on the first day, Jane's heart sank. They were dirty, loud, and rebellious. Some were obviously on drugs. Others were in trouble with the law. They had all been in school some nine years and couldn't read. How was she going to be able to teach them?

"It was obvious to me that these kids didn't feel good about themselves. They were living according to a script that said, 'I'm no good, I can't learn, no one wants me to be in school. I'll survive by being tough and mean. Or I'll drop out.' The first thing I had to do was to change their perceptions of themselves. I decided that I would find one good thing about them each day and compliment them on it," she remembers.

"Sometimes it was hard to find something good. I told them, 'You look so clean today. Thank you for taking a bath.' Or, 'You brought the book back to class. That's great.' Or, 'That's a lovely picture you drew.' Every day each student experienced the feeling of suc-cess. By the end of the year, two had gone to prison, but the other ten could read."

You, too, may have written a script that said you were a failure because you have listened to the accu-sations, criticisms, and put-downs of well-meaning par-ents, teachers, and others. You may have taken on guilt for unfortunate things that happened in your childhood for which you had no responsibility. If so, you may have an image of yourself as being bad, dumb, or the one who always fails. To change your script, use the First POWER Tool and pledge to see yourself as worthy of receiving a compliment from yourself every day. Why not set a goal of telling yourself one thing each day that you have done that was good?

Learn to turn off words others use to put you down. If someone came up to you and said, "Hey, your hair is green," you probably wouldn't believe it. You would say, "Thanks for sharing your perception with me," chuckle, and think no more about it. That's the way to treat all the other comments you hear about yourself that you know aren't true.

If many people come up and tell you your hair is green, however, you had better take a look in the mirror. There's a good chance that it is, and you will want to know so that you can *change* the color.

With a positive mental attitude, you can accept your warts and your dimples, see the good in both, and *expect* to enjoy life to the fullest.

Read Yourself Out of the Prison of Your Thoughts

We believe that the things you read have a lot to do with negative thinking. We spend the first few moments of our day reading books that will inspire us and make us feel so good about ourselves that we can't wait to get out and get going. Our favorites are Napoleon Hill's *Think and Grow Rich*, Maxwell Maltz's *Psychocybernetics*, Zig Ziglar's *See You at the Top*, Norman Vincent Peale's *The Power of Positive Thinking*, and many of Robert Schuller's books. We also read Scripture every morning, and find Matthew 5–7 especially helpful.

It's equally important for you to *avoid* reading negative material. If you're trying to meet this need, you may temporarily want to stop reading the front page of the newspaper with its detailed stories of gory accidents, depressing war reports, and conflicts of all kinds. The same goes for TV and radio news. Just shut them all off until you've learned not to answer the phone when Mr. Negative calls.

The Power of Positive Expectancy

"All things are possible to him who believes," Jesus promised the father who begged for his son to be cured of convulsions (Mark 9:23). The father could only reply, "I believe; help my unbelief." If you can conjure up positive thoughts and still not believe that good things can happen to you, you need to develop what we call "positive expectancy." Dream big dreams. Trust that great things will happen to you, and they will. It really is as simple as that.

When Jane attended the 1987 Creative Management Symposium in San Francisco, she heard Dr. Robert Schuller tell the story of how positive expectancy made his beautiful Crystal Cathedral a reality. As she recalls his telling it, when he first conceived the idea for a house of worship made of glass, Dr. Schuller's architect told him, "You're asking for the impossible." Dr. Schuller only smiled, handed him his dictionary, and asked him to look up the meaning of *impossible*. The architect thumbed through the book and then looked up in surprise.

"Dr. Schuller, there's a hole in this page. The word *impossible* has been cut out." With a twinkle in his eye, the famous preacher answered, "I know. I cut it out, because there's no such thing." The Crystal Cathedral stands today as proof that Dr. Schuller's "possibility thinking" really works.

What do you do if you can't believe that good things will happen to you? Use the Third POWER Tool's techniques. Set your goals. Then pray, asking as if you have already received the good things you want. Visualize the result of reaching those goals. Affirm that the changes you want have already occurred. When you pray and meditate in this way, you develop an *expectancy* that changes will occur. Your feelings are changed, and so are your thoughts.

Place Your Order for the Life You Want

If it is hard for you to have this kind of faith, just pretend that you have placed an order through the Sears catalog. You haven't received it yet, and you may not know exactly how or when it is going to arrive, but you know it is on the way.

After Jane's divorce, she did a lot of thinking about the qualities she considered desirable in a husband. She wrote down thirty-two things she wanted in a man. Her friends said, "I don't think you'll find all that," but Jane kept on believing there was such a partner for her. She prayed, visualized, and affirmed that such a man would come into her life. When she met Bob, she found that he had thirty of the thirty-two qualities she wanted.

If you don't put your order in, however, you can't receive the things you want. If you are a negative thinker, you may not be in the habit of dreaming dreams.

Is it hard for you to believe that good things can happen to you? Is it easier to stay stuck than to set goals, believe in them, and expect to realize them and find Life Plus? Jesus said, "Ask and it will be given you, seek and you will find, knock and it will be opened to you" (Matthew 7:7). God wants you to achieve great things. We know from experience that this is true.

Chopping Wood and Carrying Water

Do you have wonderful dreams that never happen? Or do you have wishes but tell yourself they could never come true for you? If so, you may be resisting the effort required to make changes. You may be afraid to risk actually getting out and chopping wood and carrying water so that you can have what you need.

Turn to a clean page in your notebook and write down exactly how you feel about your job, your relationships, and your physical health. Are you happy? Fulfilled? Distressed? Angry? Realize that *you are exactly where you want to be*. Not true? Then who made the decisions to put you where you are?

If you dig in your heels and refuse to risk, you can block the wonderful results that await you. You must be willing to *act* rather than *re*act. When Jane set out to obtain her master's degree, she was taking action on a goal that might have seemed unrealistic. Besides teaching full time, she had family responsibilities. Thirty-six hours of college courses and a thesis to write seemed like an overwhelming task. But she held in her mind a visualization of herself in cap and gown receiving her diploma. Finally the vision came true.

"That doesn't mean I didn't have to work for it. Sometimes I was so tired I couldn't even wiggle. I put off writing my thesis for two years. Only my visualization gave me the motivation and the extra zip I needed to do what I had to do," she says.

Jesus tells us to "seek" and "knock." By taking risks, you make good things happen. You may take a wrong path, make a mistake, or have an outright failure, but that's okay. The good in mistakes is that they help you learn. If you maintain an attitude of positive expectancy and do your part in taking risks, you will be rewarded.

Consider the number of times that athletes attempt to vault higher or throw a discus farther before they win an Olympic gold medal. At first they fail many more times than they succeed. These athletes report that the last 1 percent of effort in achieving such proficiency requires as much determination and drive as the first 99 percent. If you are attempting change, you may make so many mistakes at first that you believe you are reinforcing the negative in your life. This is not true. When you first tried to walk, you fell down more than you stood, but you wanted to walk so badly that you overlooked your failures. And you did learn to walk! Hold on to your belief that you are a person who deserves success. Hold on to your dreams. Then step out and risk.

The Automatic Reach-Out

Once you have developed a positive expectancy for yourself, your enthusiasm and helpfulness will automatically carry over to others. As you receive positive feedback from those whom you help, your self-image improves. You become able to do even greater things.

One day Jane and her former partner, Vickie, were in Houston, scheduled to return home on a noon flight that was cancelled because of an ice storm that was in progress in Dallas. Wanting very badly to return, they decided to rent a car, but neither had experience driving on slippery highways. Vickie went into the waiting area and began asking if anyone who knew how to maneuver on the ice would be willing to split the cost of the car and do the driving. One man volunteered. During the

seven hours it took him to drive the 230 miles, he had
plenty of time to tell them that he was a recovering
alcoholic who had left his wife of twenty-five years only
three months before because she continued to drink.
He loved her very much and wondered what he should
do. Throughout the long trip, Jane and Vickie were
able to reach out, encourage him, and also give him
the benefit of their knowledge. Jane told him that Bob's
second book, *Beyond Fear*, has a chapter about the
relationship between agoraphobia and alcoholism in
many people. The discomfort that some recovering alcoholics think is withdrawal symptoms really stems from
panic attacks. The approach to giving up alcohol is different for these people.

"This man was really grateful to have our input. I
don't believe that it was an accident that out of a whole
roomful of people, he was the one who drove the car,
or that we were the ones who had just the information
that would help him," Jane says. "I discovered that I
could reach out to people almost anywhere."

We can think of countless corporations that don't wait
for coincidences before they reach out to their employees and clients. Disneyland, for instance, has a pol-
icy of treating visitors like honored guests. A woman
at one of Jane's seminars told how her family had been
so excited at arriving at the famous amusement park
that she had inadvertently locked the car with the engine
still running. Then all of them left to see the sights.
Hours later they returned, their feet aching. On their
car they found a message telling them that the Disney
personnel had found the car running, made a key, un-
locked the door, and turned off the engine. Because so
many guests make the same mistake, Disneyland even
has a lock shop on the premises. Little wonder that the
parks are so famous!

You don't have to wait for coincidences before you reach out to others, either. Start participating in support groups or in prayer groups. Encourage others to think positively by telling them about the growth you see in them when misfortunes occur.

Oh Say, Do You See?

Consider the stories of two people we have heard about. One walked into a small-town cafe and noted the headline on a newspaper that was lying on a chair. It read, "Hard times are coming." This customer didn't know that the newspaper was an outdated one that the owner of the cafe had found on a dusty shelf and tossed aside. He panicked. "If hard times are coming, I'd better not build that house I wanted," he told himself. He called the construction company and said, "Hard times are coming. I'm going to have to cancel my order." The construction company owner thought, "Hard times? I'd better cancel my order for lumber." When he did, the lumber company laid off workers. Soon the town was paralyzed with fear and economic hardship, all because one man had a negative thought that led to negative feelings and negative action.

The other story is of an old woman who was in a strange village and couldn't return home before dark. She went from door to door asking if someone would let her have a bed for the night. Everyone turned her down. At last she went to the top of a hill, where she saw a big tree that would protect her. She drew her cloak around her and went to sleep. In the night, bright moonlight awoke her. Looking up, she discovered with amazement that the tree above her was covered with beautiful blossoms, for it was a night-blooming cherry. The sight of the moonlight shining through the blossom-laden branches was so beautiful that she got down on her knees and thanked God that she didn't have to sleep under a roof.

Which kind of person arc you?

9

Boosting Your Productivity —The Fifth Human Need

Have you ever been so burned-out in your job that just getting over the hump becomes your goal in life? Jane felt that way after she had taught school for many years. Every morning she got up with the thought "How many days till Friday?"

"Wednesday was the over-the-hump day for me. I even looked forward to the over-the-hump *minute*— eleven-twenty A.M.—every day," Jane says. Gone was her motivation to accomplish great things. When school let out, she congratulated herself if she had been able to perform work that was only average. Everything else in life seemed dreary, too. Her body reacted with daily aches and pains and an annual case of the flu in February. Jane was not meeting her need for feeling productive. True, she was teaching children practical skills. She was functioning in a profession that many find rewarding, but she did not *feel* useful or successful. She felt depressed. "It was as if I were on a raft without a paddle, drifting with the current to places I didn't want to go," she says.

Just as birds fly south and squirrels store nuts for the winter, human beings have an instinct for success, usefulness, and accomplishment. If you lack a sense of purpose in life, if you're dissatisfied with your progress on the job or if you feel unappreciated for your daily efforts, you are not meeting your need to feel productive. If so, you may get stuck in unchallenging careers, unhappy relationships, psychosomatic illness, and poor self-esteem.

Now that Jane is in a profession she loves, time flies. "You mean it's Friday already? I don't get to go to work tomorrow?" is her feeling. During the six years she has been in public speaking, she has never missed a speech because of illness.

That's how good you feel when you meet your need for productivity. Your job doesn't have to be glamorous or important as the world sees it, but you have to perceive it that way. It should make you feel alive, excited, and bubbly.

A Federal Express delivery person told us he loved his job. "It's like a game, trying to get everything delivered by ten-thirty A.M.," he said. "We have a ninety-nine percent success rate to uphold. Besides, I get a bonus every time I deliver something on time." He knew that without his best efforts, his company could not achieve success. Consequently he found challenge and excitement in a job many would consider low on the ladder of achievement.

We asked the cashiers at the Stew Leonard supermarket in Norwalk, Connecticut, how they felt about their jobs. They said they felt great. "We are a full-service grocery store and we care about the people," they explained. We could see what they meant. Happy customers in the check-out lines were being served ice cream and cake so they wouldn't mind waiting. Photos of 60,000 people who have shopped Stew Leonard's covered the back wall. Mr. Leonard himself strolled up and down the aisles asking everyone how he could make grocery shopping more pleasant. The enthusiasm that this enlightened merchant had for serving others carried over to his employees. They wanted to be a part of something they saw was good.

What Is This Thing Called Productivity?

Webster's Dictionary defines being productive as having the "quality or power of producing, especially in abundance; being effective in bringing about; yielding or furnishing results, benefits, or profits." Our definition is broader. We think productivity is having a purpose that you can get excited about. It is feeling useful.

Through leading Life Plus human development seminars for companies all over the United States, Jane has learned a secret about worker efficiency. She finds that productivity is often the result of ordinary people doing something a little bit extra to become superior. And it can also mean people who are a little bit out of the ordinary using their talents to the hilt. The lives of two Dallas millionaires prove this is so.

Trammel Crow's life seemed to start out in an ordinary way, according to a January 20, 1988, *Dallas Times-Herald* article. The fifth of eight children born to a bookkeeper, Crow graduated from high school and attended college at night. When he started building warehouses, they were good ones, but nothing grand. Crow theorized, however, that lots of major companies needed a Southwestern base from which to wholesale their goods, so in 1955 he took a risk and constructed the Decorative Center, a beautiful showcase for home furnishings. It was so successful that he built another wholesaling building. Others followed. Now he has eight architecturally outstanding buildings in the 9.2-million-square-foot Dallas Market Center complex, which in turn has made Dallas a major distribution area in the United States. Jane was impressed when she attended a meeting for Crow's employees in which she heard him say, "History will record that our commitment and determination to become the *best that we can be this day* will directly contribute to our becoming the strongest company in the country."

When Ross Perot left IBM to found Electronic Data Systems Corporation, his dream, according to Ken Follett's book *On Wings of Eagles*, was not to make a lot of money but to build a successful business that would employ thousands of people. Follett tells how EDS's success made Perot a multimillionaire, an employer who cared so much for his employees that he did what the U.S. government could not do—he planned and carried out a daring mission to rescue two of them from imprisonment in Iran.

When you are feeling productive, the same opportunities for great accomplishment open to you. Will you reap a financial bonanza? You may or you may not. If you don't, you're still way ahead, in our opinion. Look at the way Howard Hughes hid from life with all his billions and you will know that money isn't everything.

Dennis Byerly, a man whom Jane knew as a child, was productive in the highest sense of the word. The finest cabinet-maker in Winston-Salem, he lived in a two-bedroom house and never made a lot of money, but he always whistled as he worked. People lined up to have Mr. Byerly make their cabinets. For fifty years, Mr. Byerly also served his church as head usher. The children in the congregation knew him as the nice man with the smiling face who always said "Good morning" and gave them a stick of Juicy Fruit chewing gum as he seated them in the sanctuary.

When Mr. Byerly died at a ripe old age, some of those children—now around fifty years old—sent a funeral wreath made of Juicy Fruit wrappers. Jane remembers that at the funeral, the minister told how he had stood in the sanctuary before the service, thinking of how he wanted to praise Mr. Byerly for all he had done. He looked at the place where his faithful head usher had always stood, and suddenly he knew what Mr. Byerly would say about that. "Don't preach about me. There'll be a lot of people here, and you will have an opportunity to talk about our Saviour," he would have said. The minister changed his message. The beautiful service before an overflowing church was a celebration of life centered on the kingdom of God.

You don't have to be a millionaire to meet your need for feeling a sense of accomplishment. Jesus said not to worry about food, clothing, and other physical necessities, because these will be yours naturally from living the right way: "Seek first his kingdom and his righteousness, and all these things shall be yours as well," he said (Matthew 6:33). By enjoying hobbies, participating in family activities, and doing volunteer work, you can *be* productive and create abundance for yourself and others. You will be laying up treasures in heaven.

How Productive Do You Feel?

The following questions about your work will help you determine whether you are feeling stuck because you have not met your need for being productive. If you are not employed, apply the questions to your daily routine. Answer true or false.

1. When I get up in the morning, I dread going to work.

2. I would be happier in my work if other people didn't prevent me from doing what I want.

3. I lack a sense of accomplishment in what I am doing.

4. Others have been promoted into positions that I should have been given.

5. The surroundings at work are bleak and depressing.

6. I have too many boring tasks to do.

7. Office politics are tearing me up.

8. My job doesn't make use of all my skills and abilities.

9. I feel conflict with coworkers or my supervisor.

10. I don't feel right about the ethical consequences of my work.

11. I don't feel that I get to participate in the decisions that affect me in the workplace.

12. I am not making as much money as I should.

If you marked most of your answers "true," then you probably are feeling unproductive on the job. You have two alternatives: You can change your job, or you can change your perceptions about your work.

A dentist we know gave up a successful practice in order to work in landscaping. "I hated going to my office every day," he explained. "I wondered why I had ever become a dentist in the first place. Then I realized that the decision for me to go to dental school was made by a seventeen-year-old (me, twenty-five years ago) and my father. What I really enjoyed was gardening. I gave up my practice. Even though I had to mow lawns and prune trees to begin in a new career, and even though I made considerably less money in the beginning, I have never been sorry. I'm happy, and I can see the value of my work."

A friend of Jane's had always vowed she would stay at home to raise her children. In an endless round of diapers, car pools, and conversations about nursery rhymes, she began to feel irritable and depressed. A part-time sales job that allowed her to use her mind and relate to adults got her unstuck.

If you are experiencing burn-out and can afford to make a job change, then do so. You don't have to live with the decisions that a seventeen-year-old made, whether you are now thirty, forty, or sixty. Colonel Sanders started his world-famous fast food franchise at the age of sixty-five. Mary Kay Ash founded the Mary Kay Cosmetics Company when she had a grown son.

If circumstances don't permit you to change your job, don't give in to apathy. Even though others may be marking time until they are liberated for the day, you can gain a sense of purpose and usefulness through perceiving your work differently.

Once a man passed by three workers who were laying bricks. "What are you doing?" he asked. "Laying brick," said the first. "Making overtime pay," said the second. But the third said, "I'm building a cathedral." Guess which one felt productive.

Finding Out Who You Are on the Job

Bob Murphey, our down-home humorist friend from Nacogdoches, Texas, says, "Everyone talks about teamwork. But after thirty-five years with the volunteer fire department, I can say, 'You can't climb a ladder as a group.'"

If you are to meet your need for feeling productive, you are the one who must make the necessary changes. Using the First POWER Tool, find out who you are and accept yourself. Then find a way to sharpen your gifts. Go on to do a little bit extra with the things about yourself that you consider only ordinary.

We can't help but think of a car salesman we heard about who sharpened his gift of consideration for others to become a super producer. A young couple told us that when they went shopping for a car with two small children on a hot day in Texas, they first met a salesperson who tried to pressure them to buy a car they couldn't afford. Then he made them wait forty-five minutes (with the children growing fussier and hungrier), while he pretended to bargain on the price with his manager. The couple left that showroom angry and on edge. At another dealership, the salesman we are talking about simply asked them how much money they had to spend and found a car at that price. Meanwhile, he brought chairs for the children to sit on and bought everyone a soft drink. He asked if there was anything else he could do to make them comfortable. Within minutes the couple had signed the papers for a new car. Returning to claim it later in the day, the couple found that the salesman had parked it in the only shady spot on the lot so that they could enjoy a cool ride home. When they complimented him on all the extras he had extended to them, he said, "I just like to treat people the way I'd want them to treat me." Then they noticed a plaque on the wall with the salesman's name on it. He had sold more cars than anyone else that month!

Take a few minutes now to ask yourself some questions about yourself. What ordinary gifts do you have for doing your job? Are you especially good at detail work? Do you get compliments for not making mistakes? Do you have a strong sense of humor, or is your particular gift that of being a peacemaker when others tend to blow up? Are you creative, always thinking of ways to do things better? Are you a leader or a follower? Single out one way in which you excel, then list five ways you can develop this "ordinary gift" to become more productive. If you are good at detail work, for instance, sign up for educational courses that require this talent so that you can progress in your company. Volunteer for jobs that require accuracy. If you are creative, focus on how you can make the work in your office flow more efficiently. If you are a follower, go out of your way to help your boss.

Now think of some aspects of your job at which you are not very good. What extra things can you do to perform better? For instance, if your typing isn't accurate, pledge to proofread every page before sending it on. If you sometimes forget to communicate with important clients, clip all your telephone messages together so that you won't lose them, and return every call before you leave the office. If you feel disorganized, buy a calendar with space for writing in important dates, and fill it in month by month. Then consult your calendar every morning before setting up your day's routine.

The point is that you are in a unique position to improve the productivity for your whole company, no matter what your job is. You can do something a little bit extra and feel good about yourself, or you can plug along with the goal of "just getting over the hump." When Jane leads a motivational seminar for a corporation, she starts by asking employees to state in about twenty-five words what the basic purpose and strategy of their company is. Sometimes they look at her as if she were speaking Gaelic. Many bank employees have never thought about the fact that their purpose is to invest deposits and trusts in such a way that they make profits for their customers and shareholders. Employees of a government agency may not realize the effect they are having on the people or businesses they are regulating. Even a department store employee may lose sight of the fact that management is selling goods and making profits through service and merchandising.

Once employees have discovered the role of their employer, Jane asks why the corporation hired them. What is their purpose, their basic strategy? What talents do they bring, and how do they use them? Many don't know that, either!

We suggest that you use the First POWER Tool to discover the purpose and strategy of your employer and yourself. What is your organization's basic goal? Does it serve a purpose that will help others earn a living? Does it protect others? Enhance their lifestyle? Bring them joy? What is your role? Where do you fit in? Do you like what your company does? If so, you have an important job to do, because you are helping accomplish that service. You can find ways to do it even better!

Productive companies help their employees understand that they have an important role. When Jane was consulting with Neiman-Marcus, the world-famous Dallas-based department store, she was impressed with its motto, "Never say 'No' at Neiman-Marcus." She discovered that with that thought in mind, employees cheerfully refunded money for returned merchandise. They were creative in making decisions that would help the company live up to its motto. The employees knew they were responsible for providing true service. Some told Jane they couldn't wait to get to work. Because they *felt* productive, they helped Neiman-Marcus build profits at a time when the economy was uncertain. And they were excited and enthusiastic about their jobs.

Dr. Robert Schuller has been heard to say, "The bottom line is never money, it's always people," and we agree. Think about the time when Mary and Joseph, returning from Jerusalem, discovered that their son, Jesus, was missing. When they finally found him in the temple, he explained, "Did you not know that I must be about my Father's business?" When you think about being productive, are you coming from the God-place in you that asks, "How am I going about my Father's business today?" Are you focusing on money instead of service, or on the task instead of the person? If so, aren't you feeling a little empty?

Right now, get your notebook and write down the names of the people with whom you work. What could you change about the way you work that would help them find happiness? How would that make you feel? What are you committed to accomplishing in your job? If your work is not satisfying and it is impossible for you to change jobs, what can you do in your spare time that will give you a sense of purpose? Consider activities that give you pleasure and plan to enjoy them. Affirm that you are a child of God who deserves to take the time to enjoy yourself.

Finding Resources to Help

When Jane had career burn-out, she stayed in a job she didn't like for a long time rather than go through the difficulties of making a change. Bob had the opposite problem. He changed jobs too many times! In fact, after graduating from college, he held six different sales positions in seven years.

"I had a fear of success. Sometimes I would work up to the position of sales manager and then do something to sabotage myself so that I could quit or be fired! Subconsciously I knew that if I made too much progress, I would have to make a lot of changes. I would have to direct other people and fulfill the responsibilities of being a sales manager. That didn't feel comfortable to me, so every time I progressed to that level I made it impossible to succeed. Ironically, each time I changed jobs, I went into the same kind of work," he says.

Bob was stuck because his self-esteem was low. When he was forced to improve his self-image to overcome agoraphobia, he found that starting a new career was an exciting thing to do. He welcomed the changes in his life.

Using the Second POWER Tool, obtain information that can help you determine whether your lack of productivity comes from burn-out or the wrong choice of a career or, like Bob, from low self-esteem. Go to an industrial psychologist or a university and ask to take a personality profile test that will indicate which kinds of jobs are best suited for you. With this information you can make a wiser decision about job changes. You can also discover gifts you might not have known about. You may find interests that you can develop into avocations.

Consider enrolling in continuing education classes in your field. A refresher course or advanced training may be just what you need to regain enthusiasm.

How to Dream Those Dreams

By the time you start to use the Third POWER Tool, you should have some ideas about how you can use your ordinary and not-so-ordinary talents to become more productive. Now take those ideas and dream your dreams. See yourself accomplishing great things and feeling good about yourself. Affirm and pray, asking as if you have already received your goals.

When we met Bo Pilgrim, he told us he was just an ordinary fourteen-year-old when he started raising chickens on his grandmother's meager farm. In fact, many would have said he was destined for failure because he worked so hard he didn't have much time for school. But Bo says he "just took to chickens." He dreamed about better, more efficient ways to raise them and get them to market. He originated the Pilgrim's Pride Corporation, which now sells thousands of chickens every day. "I don't have to worry about not having a good education, because I have Ph.D.s working for me. Any time I want to know something, I just pick up the phone and ask them," he says.

Would you like to feel productive? Can you picture the results vividly? Have you asked God to help you achieve those results while holding the picture in your mind? Have you affirmed that God wants you to have this good thing?

Risking Productivity

Lots of people dream great dreams, both at night and during the day, but never accomplish anything. How do you use the Fourth POWER Tool and actually *risk doing something* to be productive?

Ed Foreman, who has taught thousands how to live productively through his Successful Life courses, told us, "Imaging and visualizing are of key importance, but if you don't get up and do something about it, you have nothing but an image." He advises getting fit so that you will have the energy to carry out your dreams. "Put more fiber into your diet; cut down on salt, sugar, fats, and cholesterol-laden foods; and do aerobic exercises for a minimum of twenty minutes every day. That will give you more energy, zest and mental sharpness than anything else I know of," he says. Foreman brought his own dreams to fruition at the age of twenty-six when he was working in the West Texas oil patch. He had an idea for a technique that would improve the drilling methods used in the salt section of the Permian Basin. It made him a millionaire. As if that weren't enough, he later became the only person to be elected congressman from two different states—Texas and New Mexico.

Dynamic Zig Ziglar advises risking self-discipline in order to become more productive. "Discipline and productivity are synonymous. When you discipline yourself to do the things you *ought* to do *when* you ought to, the day will come when you can do the things you *want* to do whenever you want," he says. He tells those who attend his seminars to take care of their health and to exercise, read good books, listen to tapes, and sleep eight hours every night so that they will be emotionally and physically ready to go to work. We feel that Zig practices what he preaches. He averages two hours a day in study and preparation for his job of encouraging others. He jogs five days a week and doesn't smoke or drink.

Yes, taking a risk means action. Set a big goal, dream about it, pray about it, and then break it down into small goals that you will be able to achieve. We'll show you how to do this in detail in the next chapter.

Another person who has taken a risk and become productive is our dentist. He promises that if he is fifteen minutes late for any appointment, he will send roses to the person who has to wait. By risking in this way, he and his staff have the motivation to keep on schedule, and if he is late, a client feels much better about the situation when the beautiful flowers arrive.

We couldn't help but be impressed by a salesman in a men's specialty store in the Highland Park Village. The weather was sunny and warm, and this shop's front door was open. As we stood near the doorway looking at a window display, the manager invited us to come in and have a glass of Perrier. We couldn't resist. As we sipped our drink, the salesman said to Bob, "You look like a sporty fellow," and began to show him clothes that would suit his personality. We ended up spending several hundred dollars simply because the salesperson took a risk by buying us a glass of Perrier!

Build on People

Like the salesman who sold Bob his new clothes, are you helping someone to look better, feel better, or accomplish more? Are you using the Fifth POWER

Tool in your job and reaching out to help others succeed?

When Mary Crowley founded Home Interiors and Gifts, Inc., she had a goal of helping women "be somebody," according to her autobiography, *You Can, Too*. She recruited and trained housewives who had no business experience to work part-time by holding sales parties in customers' homes. Many went on to make executive-level incomes, while the company's annual sales surged over the $1 million mark in a few short years. She also set up a special division of the company for the purpose of employing the handicapped.

"It was and is my theory that if you build the people, the people will build the business. If you help other people get what they want out of life, then you will get what you want out of life," Crowley maintains. She not only transformed her employees' lives, but she reached out to donate thousands of dollars to many good causes.

Is *Your* Light Shining?

"Let your light so shine before men, that they may see your good works and give glory to your Father who is in heaven" (Matthew 5:16). God has given every human being a special light, but lots of people hide it under a bushel basket. Are you letting your light shine? When you have met your need for feeling productive, you, too, can do glorious things for yourself and others.

10

Becoming Self-Disciplined —The Sixth Human Need

When Bob began to recover from his agoraphobia, he saw many things about himself that he wanted to improve. He had been a negative person. Now he wanted to think positively. Overweight and saddled with high cholesterol and triglycerides, he wanted to become physically fit. Unfulfilled in his career, he wanted to become a professional speaker. He had felt stuck a long time in many ways, but he didn't know what to do to change.

"Every time I started down the road to self-improvement, nothing seemed to happen. I would make a little progress, but when I hit some kind of obstacle, I would quit," Bob says. "Not until I met my need for being self-disciplined could I change my habits."

After Bob learned how to keep on keeping on, he was able to monitor his negative thoughts and replace them with affirmations. He stuck to his Sensible Eating Plan and aerobically conditioned his body until he could run a half marathon. He participated in weekly Toastmaster International meetings until he learned to speak effectively without fear.

Did he meet any obstacles along the way? Of course. Did he sometimes try and fail? Lots of times. Was he tempted to say, "Oh, what's the use?" and give up? Yes. Was it a lot of work? You'd better believe it! Then how did he get this kind of self-discipline? For the first time in his life, Bob learned to set goals and achieve them.

Bob isn't the only one for whom goal-setting has resulted in a changed life. We know people who have gotten unstuck from drinking or smoking or overeating by setting goals. Others have improved relationships, advanced in their careers, and overcome anxiety and depression. All of this change required daily, sometimes minute-by-minute decisions to keep on keeping on. That is why we are convinced that self-discipline is a basic human need. Without it, you can't make the changes you must make to achieve Life Plus.

If you don't have self-discipline (and most of us aren't born with it), don't despair. You can develop it by setting goals to accomplish all kinds of wonderful things and then working to achieve them. Miraculous things then just seem to happen.

Once Bob had an idea for a goal that seemed too fantastic to be achieved. He wanted to write a book that would help other people overcome agoraphobia and live the Life Plus way, but he had no journalistic talents. In fact, he couldn't even read his own writing! As for his spelling, it could only be termed imaginative. Still, he believed in goals, so he wrote this one down. When he prayed, he saw himself with a book showing his name as the author. Soon afterward, Pauline Neff heard him make a speech on agoraphobia at a Toast-masters meeting. She was already the author of books that helped people, and now she had a goal to write another one. To Bob's amazement, *she* proposed a collaboration! Together they wrote *Anxiety and Panic Attacks*, a best-seller that has helped thousands.

Bob and Pauline both feel that it was not just a coincidence that they came to know each other through Toastmasters. Their strongly articulated goals had somehow accessed a power that brought them together.

Jesus said, "If you have faith as a grain of mustard seed, you will say to this mountain, 'Move hence to yonder place,' and it will move; and nothing will be impossible to you" (Matthew 17:20). When you set goals and act on them, you are demonstrating your desire to achieve something good as well as your belief that God wants you to have it and will help you get it. Because of your faith, you are rewarded with self-discipline and sometimes even with miracles.

A Six-Point Formula for Achieving Your Goals

The kind of goal-setting we are talking about is more than just writing down a wish, setting it aside, and waiting for it to happen. Here's our six-point formula for making goals happen.

1. *Start with a burning desire.* According to Maxwell Maltz, author of *Psychocybernetics*, your goal must be more than a wish or a want. You have to desire it with all your heart and soul. The reason for this is the tremendous power your unconscious mind has over your actions. Whenever there is any conflict between the unconscious and the conscious, the unconscious always wins, hands down. You can tell yourself rationally, "I

want to stop smoking," or "lose weight," or "study harder," but unless your unconscious changes, it keeps on playing old tapes that tell you, "Oh no, *you* can't change. *You're* not that way."

Where does your unconscious get its direction? You, yourself, program it to think positively or negatively, calmly or with anxiety, starting with the emotions you felt as a child. Throughout adulthood it continues to send you the same emotions. For instance, your conscious mind can think, "I will not be afraid to assert myself and say no when my coworker pushes her work onto me." But when she hands you a big stack of reports to process, you take them without a word, work overtime, and then feel upset with yourself. Why don't you stand up for your rights? Probably because as a child you were punished (rightly or wrongly) for asserting yourself. The four-year-old you were then took this punishment as a sign that Mommy or Daddy didn't love you when you boldly pursued what you wanted. You were deathly afraid of losing their love, and your unconscious got the message. It decided to protect you with feelings of fear each time you tried to assert yourself. That is why you now allow your coworker to take advantage of you. The feelings of fear, inappropriate though they may be, have been programmed into your unconscious.

You can *reprogram* your unconscious by using emotions such as the kind of burning desire we are talking about. When you want something so badly that you can see it, feel it, and taste it, your unconscious listens and changes your self-talk. Then when your coworker approaches, your unconscious tells you, "Of course you can say no. You deserve it." (If you don't have a burning desire, we'll show you in the next section how to create one.)

2. *Write your goal in the present tense*, not in the future, and in positive rather than negative terms. For instance, do not write, "I *will be* an assertive person from now on," or "I *want to be* an assertive person." Instead word your goal, "I *am* an assertive person." Avoid negatives like *not* or *no*. Rather than stating your goal as "I will *not* smoke any more," write, "I *enjoy* being free of cigarettes today." Why do this? Your unconscious listens for the negative or positive emotions. A *no* or a *not* registers more strongly than the content of the statement. By phrasing your goal in positive, present terms, you send a message to your unconscious that you are already the way you want to be. It, in turn, will send you the appropriate feelings about your habit.

3. *Write down the benefits* you will receive if you reach your goal. For instance, say, "Now that I have stopped smoking, my body feels healthier. I am saving money. My breath is fresher. I feel wonderful!" By writing the benefits, you reinforce them in your unconscious.

4. *Break your long-term goal into subgoals*. Almost any goal can seem overwhelming if you think you have to accomplish it all in one day. It is better to make a long-term goal, then break it down into many smaller goals that you can achieve in a short time. For instance, if you must lose fifty pounds, make a subgoal of losing a few ounces every day. Your unconscious can believe in ounces. It will send you the feelings of confidence that you need in order to keep on your diet.

5. *Write down any obstacles* you can imagine that may stand in your way. For example, if you want to go back to school and get a degree, is money a problem? Is time? Are your family's feelings? Write these down, and then write out solutions for each one. If money is a problem,

can you get a loan, sell something you own, or work part-time? Writing down obstacles in advance causes you to think of solutions and avoid later emergencies. You actually see yourself handling these hurdles easily. In this way, you lessen the risk of becoming discouraged when the first obstacle actually presents itself.

6. *Make a checklist of your daily subgoals.* Monitor your progress each day right before you go to bed. If you have achieved your subgoal (or even if you have tried but failed), write down "Attaboy!" or "Attagirl!" on your calendar. Also record weekly and monthly progress. Reward yourself with an inexpensive treat, such as going to a movie you've wanted to see or buying a new lipstick (but not food!) for accomplishing bigger goals.

In his book, *Peak Performance*, Charles Garfield describes the experience of being on NASA's team to put the first man on the moon. As he recalls it, he and his coworkers seemed able to accomplish tremendous feats. They were just ordinary people, but in working to achieve this goal, he noticed that they worked long hours, solved problems, and made it to the moon. Without this team's burning desire to accomplish a goal that was great and good and a benefit to humankind, would the stars and stripes have been the first flag planted on the moon?

What Is Your Burning Desire?

If we have convinced you that you can get unstuck from almost any problem you face by meeting your inherent need to set and achieve goals . . . if you want to learn how to *develop* a burning desire, and find Life Plus, then here is an exercise for you. At the top of a clean sheet of paper in your notebook, draw a push-button. Then write your autobiography as if you were eighty-five years old, looking back over your life's accomplishments. Dream big dreams! Be extravagant about the wonderful things that you did. Whenever you have an idea for something to include and a voice inside of you says, "You could never do that," *push the button*! Know that the push-button will make it possible for you to have that experience. Then go ahead and write it down.

After you have finished, review your accomplishments. These are things that you really want in life. You could get along without them, sure, but you couldn't write this kind of autobiography when you get to be eighty-five! You can achieve all these wonderful things if you meet your need for self-discipline by practicing goal-setting and achieving.

Phil Carpenter lost the use of his legs in a water-skiing accident in 1972 and was confined to a wheelchair. It would have been easy to let all his dreams die. He didn't. "I sought out positive people who did great things," Phil told us. He began to set goals to accomplish wonderful things despite his disability. In 1981, through a lot of self-discipline, he achieved an amazing goal. He became the first person to push himself across the entire United States in a wheelchair!

"I was really tired each one of the one hundred ten days it took to push myself from Los Angeles to New York. If I had spent a lot of time worrying about problems that might happen, I couldn't have done it. Instead, I made it a point to take it one day at a time," Phil said.

By achieving this goal, other doors opened for him. He became a household name in the world of wheelchair racing and was twice a member of the United States–Pan American Wheelchair Racing team. Medical experts invited him to make speeches at rehabilitation hospitals and before scientific groups. From Phil, we have learned never to eliminate a dream, no matter how outrageously impossible it may seem.

If you're not in the habit of dreaming big dreams, play the "What do you want?" game that Jane did at a seminar she attended. Everyone selected a partner. Then, no matter what one person said he or she wanted, the partner's response was simply "But what do you really want?" The game continued for a full, frustrating thirty minutes. People started by saying they wanted a new dress or car, a trip to Tahiti, a different nose or curly hair, or a billion dollars. Then, as their partners' relentless "But what do you *really* want?" continued, they began to be angry and frustrated. Finally, at the end of the half hour, most concluded that deep down their real desire was to love themselves and to be loved. Their heartfelt wishes had been buried below the desires they thought they had.

If you can find a partner, have fun playing this game. If you don't have a partner, then look at your autobiography and write down fifty things you want to accomplish in your lifetime, no matter how impossible they seem. Now look at your list and eliminate any that are *entirely* unrealistic (but think about the way Phil Carpenter overcame realities before you do). Now select the top six items on your list. Would you be willing to work on any of these goals? If so, choose the two that cause you to feel most excited. You may not have the burning desire to put people on the moon that inspired Charles Garfield, but by this process of elimination, you have found goals that do hold a lot of interest for you. Using the six steps above, make a goal sheet for each one. Then write a daily checklist for achieving subgoals. Jane knows from experience that when you get in the habit of setting goals, you accomplish great things that you would never even have tried to do otherwise.

"People are always asking me how I, a schoolteacher from North Carolina, am suddenly able to lead seminars for major corporations and speak on nationally televised programs," says Jane. "I tell them, 'By setting goals.'"

Her first job at Feedback Plus was to sell tapes that the former owner had made of his seminar speeches. The dream of becoming a professional speaker like her boss became a burning desire. Jane also decided she wanted to become a partner in the firm. In December she wrote down these goals. By March she had used her teacher retirement funds and life savings to reach one of them. She became a partner.

At the same time, she embarked on her goal of becoming a professional speaker. One day, while visiting Los Angeles to speak at a dry cleaners' association meeting, she took time off to visit the Crystal Cathedral. Robert Schuller's guests that day included a movie star and a vocalist from England.

"I was nobody important at that point and Schuller's guests had international fame," Jane remembers, "but somehow I just knew that someday (although I didn't know how it was going to happen) I was going to be there in the Crystal Cathedral as Robert Schuller's guest. The feeling was so strong that I sat through the service *twice*. Then I went home and wrote down, 'I am Robert Schuller's guest on the "Hour of Power," and the words that I share are impacting the lives of others for good.' I read that goal every day and kept on making speeches, taking every opportunity I could to make myself known.

"After appearing on the nationally televised motivational show 'DAWN,' the producer gave me a real break. He sent a tape of me to Schuller's staff, which was seeking a woman to speak at Dr. Schuller's Possibility Luncheons.

"According to the producer," Jane recalls, "at the time the staff was viewing my tape, Dr. Schuller walked by and saw it. He said, 'Don't use her for the Possibility Luncheon. I may want her for the show.'

"Not until a year later did I get that call from Los Angeles, and it wasn't to be on the show. It was to speak at Dr. Schuller's Creative Management Symposium. I, the North Carolina schoolteacher, was to be on a panel with industrialist and philanthropist Armand Hammer, the chairman of the board of W. R. Grace Corporation, Peter Grace, and Irene Kassorla, psychologist and author of *Go for It*.

"My speech was scheduled for two small workshop sessions. I wanted to make it the best that I was capable of, so I took time to go into the Cathedral and pray that God would help me. Then I went to my session and gave the first speech. No microphone had been provided, yet I was able to project my voice with no problem. The fifty people who didn't quite fill the room gave me a standing ovation. My second workshop in the afternoon was jam-packed. Over a hundred people spilled out into the hall, trying to hear me. Shortly after that I received my invitation to be Robert Schuller's guest on the 'Hour of Power.' "

Yes, your goals may seem far beyond your reach, but if they will serve a good purpose and if you have a burning desire, you can achieve them. You may not always know how they are going to come about. You just have to have faith that they will. Our POWER tools will help you maintain the necessary self-discipline.

Being Kind to Yourself

Use the First POWER Tool to help you pledge that you are a worthy person even when you make mistakes and your self-discipline isn't as strong as it could be.

How do you react when you consume more calories than you allot for your daily goal? Smoke that cigarette you don't want to smoke? Fail to finish that report on time? Give in and yell at the children? Do you tell yourself you are a miserable failure and that you just don't have what it takes to achieve your goals? If so, you have not fully met your need for feeling beautiful on the inside. No matter how many times you try and fail, you are still a worthy person. In fact, failure is an important part of meeting a goal. When you forgive yourself and continue to work on the goal, failure is only temporary.

Consider these facts: The Beatles, according to *The Love You Make, an Insider's Story of the Beatles*, were turned down by Decca, Pye, Philips, Columbia, and HMV record companies before they went on to revolutionize popular music. Chester Carlson, who invented xerography and the copying machine, couldn't sell his invention to the first seven corporations he approached, according to a story in the February 7, 1988, issue of the *Dallas Morning News*. Eventually he made $200 million in royalties on his invention. Vincent Van Gogh sold only one painting in his whole life, and that was to his brother, yet today his paintings are worth millions. We could go on and on with stories of failure that later turned into successes. The beloved opera *Madame Butterfly* flopped at its first performance. Thomas Edison, who had invented the light bulb, forecast that talking pictures would never be successful. When Bell Telephone offered the rights to the telephone to Western Union for $100,000, Western Union refused the offer because its officers didn't believe that these new-fangled telephones would catch on!

Bob always tells agoraphobics that if they leave their homes and have a panic attack, they are to give themselves "Attaboys" and "Attagirls" even so. The reward is for *risking new behavior* rather than for succeeding.

If you are to develop self-discipline, you must quit putting your energy into thoughts of failure, giving up, self-criticism, doubt, and fear. Accept the fact that God forgives you even when you try and fail. Can you do less?

Information—A Shortcut to Effort

By using the Second POWER Tool to obtain information, you can take creative approaches to achieving goals.

A man walking beside a raging mountain river saw a small girl playing on the other side. He thought it dangerous for her to be climbing on the moss-covered boulder. Why didn't her mother come and take her off the slippery rock? Suddenly he realized that no adults were near her. She was edging closer to the place where she would surely fall into the raging torrent. The man quickly pulled off his shoes, plunged into the icy stream, swam to the other side, and pulled the little girl off the rock. Then, as he stood shivering and wet, he noticed a footbridge crossing the river only a few feet away!

Many people set goals but fail to use the Second POWER Tool. They plunge into a torrent of activity without taking time to obtain readily available information that could save a lot of effort. Be creative in seeking out such sources. For instance, if you want to change jobs, you can find helpful books, talk to personnel directors, take community college courses, and network with your friends. If your goal is to become physically fit, you can read books on how to condition yourself aerobically, or consult with a YMCA or health center. By tapping into sources of expertise, you can find shortcuts to your goal.

The more you let people know that you have set a goal, the more likely it is that you will receive creative suggestions. Find a friend who believes that you can achieve your goal and will call you each day to cheer you on. Tell friends, family, and colleagues what you have set out to do. Helpful suggestions will come from the most unlikely places as people are energized by the level of your enthusiasm.

Be open to suggestions. Recently a big eighteen-wheeler became wedged underneath a low bridge built over a freeway, and traffic was stacked up for miles. Tow trucks tried to push or pull it out but couldn't budge it. No one could figure out how to get it unstuck. Then a small boy walked up to the man with the tow truck.

"Mister, why don't you let the air out of the tires?" he suggested. Within minutes, the truck had eighteen very flat tires, but it was creeping out from under the bridge.

A suggestion to take a step backward in order to move forward may *sound* as if you are being advised to let the air out of your own tires. For instance, a job counselor may advise taking a lower-paying job or enrolling in some college courses in order to advance. If the advice seems sound, don't worry about the tires. It's better to move forward slowly than to remain stuck.

This ... or Something Better

Before Bob learned to use the techniques of change in the Third POWER Tool, he would head for the golf course telling himself that he was going to play better than ever, *but* videos of all the times the ball had gone into the rough kept playing in his head. Then when he teed off, something always seemed to happen to his swing to prevent him from making good shots. Once he learned how to visualize, he stopped thinking about his mistakes. He began to picture the ball heading straight for the green. He relaxed and stopped trying so hard to control his muscles. His game improved considerably.

Before setting out to achieve your goals, ask yourself these questions: Am I visualizing myself acting in positive ways or in the ways in which I have failed in the past? Am I affirming that I am worthy to achieve this goal? Am I thanking God that he wants to give me good things and that *I have already achieved the goal I am working on*?

We use prayer as a way to bind us back to the source from which all good things come, the God who is inside, outside, and all around us. When we set a goal that will work for the benefit of mankind, we create a true master-minding alliance with God, who acts through the thoughts and actions of man.

"He who believes in me will also do the works that I do; and greater works than these will he do, because I go to the Father," Jesus said (John 14:12).

We know from experience, however, that God moves in mysterious ways. We believe that you have to be careful what you pray for, because you might get it! You might stand in God's way of giving you something that would be much better than you could have imagined. So, just as Bob presented his wishes about improving at golf and then *released control* over his golf swing, we present our wishes, then turn them over to God to act on them as he wills. We pray, "This, Lord, or something better."

Our love story is a good example of what happens when you release through prayer the behavior that stands in the way of your getting unstuck. We had been dating seriously and then broke up. When we saw each other at Professional Speaker Association meetings, we ignored each other. Both of us were miserable, and both of us turned to God for help.

Jane says, "When I prayed, I had the feeling of letting go of all my anger at Bob. I told God, 'If it is your will for us to be apart, then I accept it and let it go.' That opened up space for creativity to come in. One night after I had refused to speak to Bob at the meeting, I did a lot of praying. Suddenly I felt I had to call Bob and tell him that I couldn't stand our not speaking any more. I phoned him and told him, 'No matter how you feel, I want you to know I still love you and want to be your friend if nothing else.'

"Bob then told me that when we broke up he had fallen off his spiritual path. He had forgotten to pray and meditate every day. Now he had been praying again and he, too, wanted to resume our friendship. We started over, and within a few weeks we decided we wanted to marry."

Have you presented your goal to God, visualized and affirmed that you are meeting your goals, and let go so that God can give you what you want—or much better?

How to Make Dust

Og Mandino, author of *Mission Success*, says, "Everyone has twenty-four hours a day to make dust in the world." You can set all the goals you want, but if you procrastinate, sleep the morning away, fill up your time with worry and fear, or throw yourself into other activities so that you won't have to work on your goals, you aren't kicking up much dust.

The Fourth POWER Tool, engaging in risk, is the one that makes the difference in whether or not you *achieve* your goals. You can set all the goals in the world, but unless you actually risk doing what you must do twenty-four hours a day to change your behavior, you can't achieve them.

Ask yourself these questions:

1. Does the day somehow get away before I have had a chance to work on my goals?

2. Do others prevent me from working on my goals?

3. Do I have so many responsibilities that there isn't any time to work on goals?

4. Am I just too busy to work on goals?

If you answered yes to any of these questions, you will benefit from learning time management techniques. Experts have many different approaches to helping you make the most efficient use of time. We want to give you a very simple rule that we learned from *Psychocybernetics*. Each morning when you get up, write down a list of the things that you want to do that day. Then set priorities. Start with your number one priority and work on it until it is finished. Then start on number two. If you don't complete your entire list, don't worry. You will at least have accomplished the things that are most important to you.

The great philosopher William James said, "Launch

a habit with commitment, practice with relentlessness, put the habit into use as soon as possible." Don't let anything interfere.

Jane tells participants in her seminars that if they say they don't have time for whatever they need to do, they are really saying, "I don't want to," or "I'm not going to take the time."

"Occasionally you may have a legitimate time crunch," she says, "but haven't you had a day when you were scheduled for every minute of your time, and then someone called to invite you to do something you really wanted to do and somehow you did it? We all find time for the things we really want to do."

When Bob works on goals, he simply tells himself he doesn't have a choice about whether he will work on them or not. "Most people don't choose whether to brush their teeth. They just do it. When you get up in the morning, don't think of having a choice about whether to work on your goals." With this philosophy, Bob attended Toastmasters meetings twice a week at 7 A.M. for two years and only missed two sessions. "I didn't really want to get up early and stand before others feeling embarrassed, but I programmed my mind with the fact that I didn't have a choice. This was what I had to do to become a professional speaker."

If a daily goal seems too overwhelming, you may need to break it down into smaller increments. When Jane was writing her thesis for her master's degree, she couldn't get started. For two years she was stuck. Finally her professor told her, "Just sit down and write, 'I can't write this, I'm not getting my mind together.' Keep on writing until finally you get out all your fear and anxiety, and then you'll be able to start. Write at least one page every day."

Jane says, "Once I made a goal to finish one page a

day, I completed my thesis within a few months."

We both caution you, however, not to get so caught up in achieving goals that you fail to have a balance in your life. At one of Jane's seminars, a very successful banking executive stood at the back of the room with tears running down his cheeks. Finally he told the group, "This morning my five-year-old said, 'I can't wait until it's the weekend so that we can hug and kiss.' I told her, 'Oh, honey, we can hug and kiss whenever we want,' but she said, 'Oh no, Daddy. You don't have time—not until Saturday.' "

Another parent told a similar story. Her five-year-old son had wanted to show her something outside and she had told him she didn't have time. "He put his hands on his hips and said, 'Mamma, just when *will* you have time?' " she said. As she related this story, she, too, started to cry. This incident had taken place twenty years before, and her grown son had become a failure in every way possible. She was torturing herself with the thought that everything would have turned out differently if she had made quality time with her family one of her priorities.

Encourage Others to Reach Their Goals

When you announce that you have started working on goals, some people will almost certainly react with a startled "You, change like that? I don't believe it!" Regrettably, your own family may react this way. Perhaps they have seen you at your worst, and they find it hard to believe that you can become the wonderful person you now want to be. Or maybe they fear that the "new you" will have no use for them. But nobody needs negative feedback! If you are getting it, then find others who do believe in you. At the same time, be especially sensitive to the needs of others who are trying to get unstuck. Use the Fifth POWER Tool, and reach out to encourage others to meet their goals.

Zig Ziglar says that if you help others achieve what they want in life, you will achieve what you want, and we believe it. Many times we have given other speakers leads and suggestions that have helped them reach a goal of becoming a better speaker. Inevitably, we receive far more help than we give.

A Thing Called Commitment

We love the story about the chicken and the pig who were walking down the road and came upon a sign in front of a cafe that said, "Bacon and Eggs, $2.99." "Wow," said the chicken, "they're advertising my eggs. That makes me feel humble and proud." "Feel the way you want to," snapped the pig. "Your part is only a contribution. Mine is a commitment."

Self-discipline does take commitment. It takes a recognition of how precious time is and a resolve to make the most of each moment. A friend of ours likes to tell a story that demonstrates what we are talking about. He says that Floyd Little of the Denver Broncos, who was only five feet eight inches tall, had been told that he was too small to play in a sport where size and weight were so important. Yet he became one of the most famous running backs of the 1970s. When his coach asked him how he managed to become a peak performer with such a disadvantage, it is said that Little replied, "Every time I touch the ball, I tell myself that it's going to be the last time I have an opportunity to run with that football. Knowing that, I want to run the very best that I can."

When you meet your need for having self-discipline, as Little has, you, too, can move mountains.

11

Gaining an Appreciation of Beauty —The Seventh Human Need

Whcn young Dr. Carl Hammerschlag began serving in the U.S. Public Health Service in the Santa Fe Indian Hospital in 1965, he discovered that his patients knew ways of healing that he had not been taught in medical school. One very old Indian named Santiago who was suffering from congestive heart failure wanted to know how Dr. Hammerschlag had learned to heal. When this Pueblo Indian priest and clan chief heard Hammerschlag's academic credentials, he was not impressed. He only smiled and said, "Do you know how to dance?"

Touched by the whimsy of the old man's query, Hammerschlag shuffled a little at his bedside. Then Santiago got out of bed and began to show him *his* way of dancing.

"You must be able to dance if you are to heal people," he said.

"And will you teach me your steps?" Hammerschlag asked, indulging the aging priest.

"Yes," Santiago said. "I can teach you my steps, but you will have to hear your own music."

In his fascinating book, *The Dancing Healers*, Hammerschlag tells how such experiences with the Indians taught him to understand that health is an ongoing process. To be truly well, you must be in tune mentally, spiritually, and physically with all that is living, including nature and other people. Dancing is one of the rituals that Indians use in order to experience awe and the presence of the infinite. Indians know that when they hear their own music, they are whole.

In America today, many of us lead fractured lives. We do not experience family closeness because of the prevalence of divorce and stress-producing work routines. We sometimes desecrate rather than revere the earth. Can busy, industrialized people reconnect with each other and nature as the Indians do? Is it possible that dancing, music, and an appreciation of beautiful things can make you healthier and more fulfilled?

An awareness of beauty is essential to a fulfilling life, not something in which to participate only if you have some spare time. Human beings have a basic need for music, dancing, poetry, drama, art, and nature. By letting beauty heighten your emotions, you can avoid being stuck, not only in sickness, but in depression, low productivity, or an "Is that all there is?" kind of feeling.

Have You Met Your Need for Enjoying Beauty?

Unfortunately, in our society, many people just never have the opportunity to study beauty. They are so busy competing, striving, and tending to the necessities of life that they don't take time to admire beautiful things that could make their hearts sing.

If you are like most men, you may never have been allowed to respond to beauty. Because you have been taught to suppress your emotions, you may think it a sign of weakness to spend time on the arts. Some men we have met can't give themselves permission to enjoy a walk in the woods unless they have a gun in their hand. That seems sad to us.

Another deterrent to enjoying beauty is the notion that you don't want to waste your precious time on nonproductive things. You just don't see any payoff.

If you think we are crazy for suggesting that you actually have a need for appreciating beauty, ask yourself these questions:

Have you ever been so depressed that spring has come and gone and you never noticed the flowers blooming? Wouldn't you rather have enjoyed them?

Have you ever been so frazzled with demands and activities that you were on the point of exploding, when suddenly you heard a piece of music that was so beautiful it brought you to the point of tears? Didn't you feel calmer and better able to do your tasks afterward?

Have you ever walked down the street feeling angry and put upon, then noticed a sunset that was so brilliant that you forgot about your troubles? Is it possible that being able to appreciate such beauty has the power to take you out of yourself to a better, happier place?

Just why are there so many different colors, sounds, textures, and tones in the world? Why are we able to move our bodies gracefully? Why do we love to see the way a horse gallops across a field? Is it possible that these elements of beauty were put into the world to awaken the creative spark within us so that we could accomplish better things?

Beauty Is Its Own Reward

The benefits of experiencing and appreciating beauty are not just in your mind. Studies show that when you take time to drink in beauty, your health improves, and you become more creative. The arts help you acknowledge your emotions of sadness so that you can go on to happiness, whether you are a performer or an observer.

In *The Arts in Psychotherapy*, music therapist Mark Rider, of Southern Methodist University, presents evidence that music enables people to effect subtle changes in their blood chemistry, including production of the all-important T-cell that is vitally linked to the body's ability to fight disease. In his research, Rider used music as a tool to enhance his subjects' therapeutic imaging. Blood samples taken before and after a twenty-minute imaging session with music showed that the subjects significantly increased their level of lymphocytes and neutrophils. Rider has also used music therapy to control pain.

The experience of Gregory Bateson, the famous British philosopher, seems to bear out this research. Jane heard a California therapist say that when Bateson discovered that he had only two weeks to live, he asked to spend his last days at Big Sur, overlooking the beautiful ocean. A friend, trying to make him comfortable and alleviate the pain from his cancer, began to play beautiful music and to massage him. Bateson, as this therapist recalled it, hurt so badly that he could only bear having a single finger stroked. After two weeks of listening to his favorite music and watching the waves from his window, however, Bateson was still alive. His friend began to stroke his hand. Time went on. When at last Bateson could tolerate a massage of his entire body, he was strong enough to sit up in bed. His friend prayed with him, massaged him, and listened to the music with him. By the end of the year, Bateson was healthy enough to dance. In fact, he lived five more years, and he danced every day, celebrating the gift of life that he had miraculously received.

An appreciation of beauty also makes you more creative. When Bob was attending Texas Tech University, he had a fraternity brother named John Deutschendorf, who obviously had musical talent but seemed unable to find an audience until he moved to Aspen, Colorado. After he drank in the beauty of snow-covered mountains and silent, fluttering aspen leaves, he composed "Rocky Mountain High," a song that brought him fame. That was when he changed his name to John Denver.

Many people find that creativity is enhanced by beauty. Fine art hanging in the offices of progressive corporations inspires executives to solve business problems. We know authors who have overcome writer's block simply by reading beautiful poetry and mothers of small children who have found more creative ways of parenting after taking up ballet as a hobby.

If you are stuck because of anger, sadness, or frustration, an appreciation of the arts can serve as a catharsis. When you identify with the tragedy of *Madame Butterfly* or *Our Town*, you can mourn your own losses and understand at a deeper level the universal meaning of the human condition. With your emotions spent, you can go on with a lifted mood to serenity.

People have survived terrible ordeals by reaching beyond themselves to what beauty they can find in their circumstances. When Jane attended an exhibit of children's art from the Holocaust at the 1978 North Carolina State Arts Consortium, she discovered that these young survivors relished a single flower that bloomed on the grounds of a death camp. Gerald Coffee, our friend who was a prisoner of war in Vietnam, said that he and the other prisoners of war tap-coded poetry to each other from their bamboo cages until their knuckles were raw in order to raise their morale. In her inspiring book *Joni*, Joni Eareckson, a quadriplegic, describes how she freed her spirit by painting beautiful pictures with a paintbrush held in her teeth. Could these people who suffered so much have continued to live if they hadn't transcended their circumstances through the arts?

We believe that an awareness of beauty can bring you closer to God. Drink in the beauty of a stained glass rose window or walk through fields of wildflowers in the spring, and you cannot help but feel at one with the creator of the universe. You will understand why David danced with joy before the Lord (II Samuel 6:14). Beauty comes from the Creator, and we in turn can only respond. We make a joyful noise before the Lord. We dance. Or we mold a graceful vase out of clay or compose moving poetry. Afterward, we are able to live and act in the world in more meaningful ways.

How We Developed an Appreciation for Beauty

Jane grew up with an appreciation of beauty in nature because her mother took her and her sister for a walk every day in the North Carolina woods close to their home. They looked for moss, picked beautiful red, yellow, and deep purple leaves in the autumn, and in summertime they hunted in the gurgling stream for rocks sparkling with shiny veins of mica.

Jane also studied ballet as a child. When she was fourteen, her parents took her to New York to see her first Broadway show, *Camelot*, starring Richard Burton, Robert Goulet, Julie Andrews, and Roddie Mac-Dowall. "I was so moved I couldn't breathe. Right then I decided that when I went to college, I wanted to study drama," she said.

In high school Jane performed in Shakespearean plays and studied dancing. She would become so involved in the music and movement that hours would pass without her realizing that her body was becoming tired. When she learned to paint and play the piano, she again was transported beyond herself, so that time meant nothing. These activities, so enjoyable in themselves, paid off with surges of energy and creativity.

Like many men, Bob has no recollection of being impressed by the fine arts as a child. He did, however, have an instinctive love of nature that later, to his surprise, helped him get unstuck from a poor golf game.

"For anyone who plays golf, Pebble Beach is like a dream come true. The first time I played there I was so excited and nervous that I duffed the very first ball. On the next shot, I hit out of bounds. I ended up with an eleven on the first hole. I kept on playing badly, until by the sixth hole I was fifteen over par. I walked up to the tee box, feeling really discouraged. Then suddenly I looked around and saw where I was. I was standing on a portion of land that hangs over Carmel Bay. The temperature was a perfect sixty-five degrees. The wind was soft and gentle. The sun was glinting on the waves, and I could actually hear sea lions barking in the water. I was overcome with the beauty of it all. When I stopped long enough to take in all the wonderful things that God had created, I just had to laugh at my golf score. It didn't seem to matter," Bob remembers.

"The strange thing is that after that, I almost hit a hole in one. When I decided to enjoy beauty rather than focus on making the best score, my game actually improved," he says.

When you take time to meet your need for appreciating the beauty around you, you will be able to get unstuck from poor performances, too. If you have never learned to enjoy the arts, try using the POWER tools to increase your appreciation of them.

You and Beauty

Using the First POWER Tool to accept yourself as you are, realize that it's all right if you don't have an appreciation for beauty. Maybe you didn't grow up with such an appreciation. Maybe you've been too busy to take time. Don't beat yourself up about it. Consider which one of the arts most appeals to you. Maybe you like to listen to rock and roll music but have never thought about learning to enjoy classical music. Perhaps you like to draw, but you have never considered studying fine art or sculpture. Maybe you dance for fun but have never dreamed of performing an interpretive dance. Or maybe, like Bob, you like nature but just never took the time to bask in it.

Once you have discovered a basic interest, write a goal in your notebook to develop it. Write, "I enjoy classical music," or "fine arts," or "interpretive dancing," or whatever you want to learn to enjoy. Then make some daily goals that will gradually lead you to develop that interest. You might write, "Today I will visit the art museum," or "Today I will sign up for a course in music appreciation or dancing." Affirm that you are a worthy person who deserves to take the time to develop these interests.

Sources to Help You Appreciate Beauty

"That man is the richest whose pleasures are the cheapest," wrote Henry David Thoreau in his *Journal*. Thoreau's two years of living with nature at Walden Pond led to his becoming a celebrated philosopher. You don't have to deplete your bank balance in order to develop an interest in beauty. You don't have to pay a cent to expose yourself to the beauty around you. Take a walk among the trees and flowers of a park. Visit the library and browse among good books. Go to the art museum and take a tour or ask a docent to explain how the old masters handled light and darkness, viewpoint, and composition in their works. Or go to a symphony concert, the ballet, or to your local theater.

You may want to take a course in art or music appreciation, in playing an instrument or learning to dance. Join a great books discussion club. These resources are available in most cities. There is no shortage of information on the arts, no matter where you live, and much of it is free.

The Techniques, Esthetics, and Serendipity

You can combine the Third POWER Tool's technique of visualization with the joyful emotions you get from beautiful things to create a powerful way of changing negative thoughts. Bob first discovered this tool, which he calls Emotional Transfusion, while recovering from agoraphobia. When he used Emotional Transfusion to replace the negative tapes in his unconscious, he was no longer afraid.

Emotional Transfusion works much like a blood transfusion. The blood donated by a healthy person adds to and enriches the blood of a sick person. In Emotional Transfusion, you transfuse *your own positive emotions to yourself* in order to vanquish negative feelings and enrich the positive in your life. For instance, Bob used to have a fear of making cold sales calls. He used Emotional Transfusion to transfuse the positive emotions he experienced at Pebble Beach into his thoughts about the dreaded sales call. He also visualized a big smile on the face of the client and saw himself as being happy, too. He affirmed, "I am enjoying talking to my client as much as I enjoyed the beauty at Pebble Beach." When he used Emotional Transfusion in preparation for making cold sales calls, his fear miraculously disappeared.

Here is a simple four-step method for using Emotional Transfusion:

1. *Go into the relaxed meditative state called alpha*—a state in which the electrical impulses in your brain cycle at the rate of about ten cycles per second. This is the normal state you are in when you are on the point of falling asleep, when you are waking up, or when you are meditating or praying and feeling very calm and relaxed. You can achieve this state by sitting comfortably, breathing deeply, and consciously relaxing each part of your body while you tell yourself you are completely relaxed. (For a complete alpha relaxation script, refer to one of Bob's other books: *Anxiety and Panic Attacks* or *Beyond Fear*.)

2. *Set up your donor visualization*. Simply visualize the most pleasant, quietly joyful scene you can remember. Use any experience that has made you feel exhilarated, happy, calm, peaceful, and capable. Many people choose something connected with nature, such as the

beauty of a lake or a spring meadow with its green trees and brilliant wildflowers. Or it may be a time when music or art transported you beyond yourself. Spend a few moments enjoying the peace and happiness you feel there.

3. *Set up your receiver visualization* while holding on to the peace and happiness. This is the scene that pictures the negative situation you want to change. Perhaps it is you interacting with an angry spouse, a demanding boss, or a difficult client. Don't spend any time dwelling on the negatives. Just bring the situation to mind.

4. *Immediately transfuse the happy, positive feelings of the donor visualization into the receiver visualization.* Feel the peace and joy from your donor visualization. Envision your angry spouse, demanding boss, or difficult client with a loving smile. Affirm, "I am enjoying talking to this person as much as I enjoyed being in _____ (the scene of your donor visualization)."

You can get unstuck from almost any activity that feels negative by using Emotional Transfusion.

Risk the Time to Enjoy Beauty

Folk wisdom advises, "Take time to smell the roses" in the midst of your daily activities. If you are stuck in any way, however, we advise you not just to take some time out to smell the roses, but to *give it your top priority*. Keep on enjoying beauty until you feel yourself lifted out of the mire. After that, you can spend time accomplishing whatever it is you need to do—and it will be a whole lot easier to do it.

Using the Fourth POWER Tool, engage in the risk of taking time to appreciate esthetics. Set a daily goal of spending at least one hour a day reading about the art you prefer, visiting a museum, or tuning in a relevant TV program. Go for a walk in the woods with children. They will show you all the beautiful things about nature close to the ground, and you can show them the wonders of the sky.

If you have a hard time becoming enthusiastic about the arts, try this experiment. Pretend you are a Martian who has just landed on Earth. Look with amazement at flowers and trees popping out of the ground. Drink in the wonderful colors of the sky, the grass, the walls of beautiful places you visit. Absorb the power of paintings and sculpture. When you hear music, listen as if you've never heard musical sounds before. Rather than taking for granted all the beauty around you, you will feel a spark of interest. Then set more goals to fan that spark into a blaze of excitement. Risk getting involved!

Reaching Out with the Arts

Using the Fifth POWER Tool can be as simple as helping others become aware of the beauty around them. You can say to a companion, "Isn't that a beautiful song?" or "Look at that beautiful sunset." Or make a point of giving something beautiful to others. When Jane was Miss Winston-Salem, she and her sister, Rebecca, took Moravian Christmas candles as presents to residents of a nursing home during the holidays. She still remembers the woman whose vacant expression changed to one of radiance when she received the lovely candle. "Oh, it must be Christmas," the woman said. Her life had been so empty that she had not even realized it was the season of giving and love until Jane and Rebecca reached out with a beautiful gift and a smile.

If you have children, by all means reach out to them

and help them develop a love of beauty and the arts. We know a woman who raised four children. Looking back, she can't remember anything about it except making beds, cooking meals, and washing clothes. She was stuck in a deadly routine and didn't know it! How much more fulfilling it would have been to hold the hands of her children and point out the flowers in a garden, to hang pictures at their eye level so they could enjoy them, to listen to "Peter and the Wolf" with them and read Robert Louis Stevenson poems together.

The Wonder of Beauty

Once Jane led a seminar for the teachers of Booker, Texas, a tiny town in the dusty, flat panhandle. Booker has one bank, one school, and one cafe. To encourage the teachers to teach an appreciation of the arts, Jane asked the teachers to bring back something beautiful to show to the others after the lunch break. Some held up paintings. One man brought his guitar and sang. One young teacher proudly showed off her six-week-old baby.

Still another woman held in her hand a tiny little brass cylinder, beautifully decorated. No one knew what it was. The teacher explained that she had bought it while visiting the Holy Land. It was a tear vessel, over a thousand years old.

"You see," said the woman, "it was the custom during Biblical times to collect tears, whether of joy or sorrow. Whenever you cried, you held the tear vessel to your eyes and scooped up the tears. Then you poured them out of the tear vessel into an urn. Throughout your lifetime you collected your tears, and when you died, your loved ones anointed your head with them before your burial. Your tears were your most precious possession."

Then she gave an explanation of something in the Bible that amazed everyone. Luke 8 recounts the famous story of the woman who was so grateful to Jesus for forgiving her many sins that she knelt and wet his feet with her tears and wiped them with her hair. "Everyone thinks that the woman cried, but what she really did was to pour out her most sacred possession, the tears she had collected from a lifetime of joy and sorrow," the teacher said.

How moved everyone was! "As we ran our fingers over the little brass cylinder, we were no longer in a tiny little Texas town on the dusty plains," Jane remembers. "We were transported over the centuries to the Holy Land, feeling the same gratitude and awe and wonder that the woman in Luke felt. We were connected to each other and all humanity in a special way that we could not explain."

Since that time Jane has seen other tear vessels in museums. She has read about them in books. She feels that her life has been deepened immeasurably through learning to appreciate this art treasure.

> " 'Beauty is truth, truth beauty,'—that is all
> Ye know on earth, and all ye need to know."

So wrote John Keats in "The Eve of St. Agnes" in the nineteenth century. It is still true today. When you meet your need for appreciating beauty, you will be true to yourself. The truth is a wonderful power for getting unstuck.

12

Becoming God-Centered —The Eighth Human Need

We will never forget how we discovered that we had not met our need for having a relationship with God. This realization, which we will always consider somewhat of a miracle, happened after we were dating. We had been instantly attracted to each other at the time we met. We became inseparable. We didn't realize, however, that the attraction was largely physical and emotional. The hunger we felt for physical closeness and emotional support after our divorces was being met, and we were exhilarated. For about three months we were in that wonderful state of being in love, even though we weren't sharing the deepest and most important part of our lives—the spiritual part. Bob was the first to realize that something was lacking.

"A voice inside of me seemed to be screaming, 'This isn't right. This isn't what you want. This isn't satisfying you.' I decided to break our relationship and hoped the break would be a friendly one. It wasn't. We ended up not speaking," he remembers.

Both of us were so stuck in anger, self-pity, and depression that we functioned far below our optimum level. We couldn't seem to heal ourselves or the breach between us. Two months later, when both of us gave this hurt over to God and prayed for each other, we were reunited. God had accomplished what we had been unable to do. This miracle of reconciliation made us realize that in order to stay together, we needed to *keep* a spiritual element in our relationship. This is why we spend the first moments of our day praying together and reading the Bible and other inspirational literature. If we have any differences, we discuss them then, at a time when we feel a oneness with God.

The changes in our lives have been so wonderful that we are convinced that a relationship with God is a need for everyone. You are a body, a mind, and a spirit. If you do not nourish the spirit, you will feel incomplete. If you are not meeting your need for being connected with the life force behind creation, you miss your chance to participate in miracles. Instead you make do with a life that is average at best, or below par. Then it is too easy to feel victimized. The life-changing events and losses that are the normal human condition become tragedies with no redeeming value.

We want to make it absolutely clear that we are talking about having a spiritual *relationship*, not just being religious. If you are religious, you may go to church every Sunday and read the Bible every day. You may know a lot *about* God, but you don't have a spiritual relationship *with* God. Once you experience this beautiful wholeness through prayer and through living your life as if a higher power is there beside you, lovingly helping you move ahead in all your activities, it carries over into everything you do. Once you are convinced that God wants you to have good things, you will see the miracles that are happening all around you. When that happens, you don't have to be stuck in any kind of circumstance.

The Thing About Miracles

According to Webster's Dictionary, a miracle is "an extraordinary event manifesting a supernatural work of God, or an extremely outstanding or unusual event, thing, or accomplishment." We believe that you can have both kinds of miracles when you are attuned to your spiritual self and in relationship with God.

In fact, Jane would not be alive today without a miracle. When she was burned so badly as a child, the doctors came to her parents on the fourth night and said, "Jane's vital signs are critical and her body has begun to turn blue. Don't go home. We don't believe she will make it through the night." Her parents, in desperation, went to the outside balcony of the hospital, got down on their knees, and prayed all night. Members of their church were praying, too.

It happened that the pediatrician who had cared for Jane since birth had been in Europe. Returning to the United States that very day, she had intended to spend some time in New York. On an impulse, however, she decided to rent a car and drive to her home, ten hours away. Arriving in Winston-Salem at two A.M., she decided on another impulse to drop by her office. She found a large pile of notes and correspondence that had accumulated in her absence. By coincidence, the first note she picked up informed her of Jane's burns. Instead of going home, she decided to go straight to the hospital. When she saw Jane, she immediately noticed what the other doctors had been unable to see: The bandages wrapped tightly around the trunk of Jane's body were causing it to swell. Jane was literally suffocating to death. The pediatrician grabbed scissors, cut off the bandages, and soaked Jane in a warm bath to restore her circulation. Jane lived!

Today Jane's parents are sure that their prayers led to the strange impulses of her pediatrician. They call Jane's survival a miracle.

We know of business miracles, too. In her inspiring book *Mary Kay*, Mary Kay Ash tells how she set a goal of building a business by the Golden Rule. She and her son started out by filling bottles and jars with beauty products in her garage while training salespeople to "do unto others what you would have them do unto you." Mary Kay Cosmetics is now among the top Fortune 400 companies, and Mary Kay rewards her international sales staff with lavish incentives such as her famous pink Cadillacs. She urges everyone in the company to "put God first, your family second, and your career third."

When you are in a relationship with God, you can perceive and benefit from everyday miracles, too. For instance, when we were in charge of a regional workshop of the National Speakers Association in San Antonio, everything started out wrong. The beautiful San Antonio River had been drained, so the hotel overlooked a muddy ditch filled with workers. We had planned a patriotic musical review to open the program, but the sound system was so bad that no one could enjoy it. Embarrassed and worried, we retreated to our room during a break. There we could have dwelled on our failures. Instead, we turned our fears of failing over to God and told him we were willing to let him do with our workshop whatever he wanted. When the meetings resumed, the whole atmosphere seemed different. We felt different. Even when the hotel filled with smoke from a fire down the street and the elevators stopped working, no one complained. We projected a spirit of joy, and a wonderful sense of community was returned to us. The whole workshop became filled with love and fun. At the end, we received the highest evaluations of any workshop ever held. What a miracle! We could have been so depressed over the poor beginning that we put a damper on everyone. Instead, when we turned our fears over to God, he made everything extra good.

Sometimes people experience what we call miracles of adversity. Bob had agoraphobia, which was a terrible disability; but because he did, he was able to help thousands of other people stop having panic attacks. With this "gift" of agoraphobia, he learned how to think positively, use his unconscious in amazing ways to get unstuck, and achieve his goals for deep and lasting self-improvement.

In her book *Tough Love*, Pauline reports the amazing things said by parents of teen-aged drug abusers after participation in a drug program that encouraged dependence on "a higher power." "I'm not glad that my son became a drug abuser, but I'm grateful that *because* he did, I have found a wonderful new way to live," said one mother. In the past she had felt hopeless and helpless about the way that bad things seemed to happen to her. Now God was helping her take responsibility for making changes. The results seemed like miracles.

Everyone can see the miraculous in a healing like Jane's or in a business success like Mary Kay's, but not everyone can see the miraculous in the way our workshop turned around or the way the parents in *Tough Love* changed. To see the everyday miracles and the miracles of adversity, you must see with the eyes of faith.

If You Don't Have Faith

Maybe you're thinking, "I go to church pretty often. I've read the Bible. I may be stuck, but it is not because I haven't met my need for a relationship with God."

Don't be too sure! A lot of people both in and out of churches believe in a Creator, but have no daily, ongoing relationship with him. This is like believing in love but not loving anyone. If what you believe in is not a part of your daily life, it doesn't do you any good. Here are three common misconceptions about having a relationship with God.

Misconception Number One: You can get along very nicely without faith. You may have this misconception if your parents failed to teach you how to see with the eyes of faith while forcing you to attend church. Or maybe they tried, but their teachings just didn't work for you.

If this is the way you feel, ask yourself why, since the beginning of recorded history, man has felt an innate need to worship something higher than himself. Why has every culture developed rituals designed to bring its people into a closer relationship with this power? Why do we sense the continuum of life in nature and in the leaves that fall from the trees and nourish other plants and yet do not sense such an enduring life force in ourselves?

Is this aspect of you that lives forever something that you are responsible for? If not, who is? If you could have more of this good life force simply by seeking to have a relationship with God, would you risk doing it?

In our own lives, we have found that we can have money, acknowledgment, and recognition and still feel very empty when we deny the God that is within us.

William J. Murray, the son of Madalyn Murray

O'Hair, tells in his revealing book *My Life Without God* of the turmoil he experienced as a child growing up with a mother who became famous for advocating atheism. As an adult his marriages failed. Even though he had a brilliant mind, he never held a job very long. He was stuck in self-defeating behavior and never realized that his real need was for God to help him transcend his own background. After working for atheistic causes all his life, he finally attended Alcoholics Anonymous, found a higher power and made a fulfilled life for himself.

Take a few moments to write in your journal a description of who you are in relation to whatever it is that you believe created you. Be truthful. Perhaps the best you can do is to write, "I believe there is a God who created the universe and me as a part of it. Even though I don't feel any personal relationship with him, I would like to."

Misconception Number Two: You are afraid that "God will get you" if you aren't perfect. Many have this faulty conception of God. They believe that he is "up there" keeping a record of every mistake and sending punishment accordingly. If this is your belief it is little wonder that you don't have a strong spiritual connection. We don't know how anyone can have this vision of God after reading in Luke 15 what Jesus said when he was criticized for being a friend to sinners. He said, "What man of you, having a hundred sheep, if he has lost one of them, does not leave the ninety-nine in the wilderness, and go after the one which is lost until he finds it?"

God is not a God who is keeping a list. He is a God who loves us anyway, even though we refuse the good things he wants to give us. Of course, there is such a thing as cause and effect. If you do something mean or ugly or if you fail to do what you know is best for you, you can only expect unpleasant consequences. For instance, if you continue smoking, you may get cancer. But God does not give you this terrible disease as a punishment. You make a mistake and reap the consequences. Meanwhile, God seeks you out like a shepherd who wants to protect and comfort his lost sheep.

Now write in your journal the ways that you believe God has punished you in this life. Then, after each statement, write out affirmations, such as "God loves me and wants to give me good things."

Misconception Number Three: God really isn't all-powerful or all-loving. Maybe you prayed for help and afterward the worst possible thing happened to you. Many people get stuck in bitterness and rage when this happens because they reason that either God wasn't powerful enough to do whatever they asked or he didn't love them enough to do it. When you suffer the loss of a loved one, a painful divorce, or any other heart-wrenching tragedy, you may not be able to see how God can still make something good out of it for you and the rest of humanity. With faith, however, you can view these painful happenings differently. Knowing that God loves you, you will understand that even though you don't yet see a good result, there will be one. It takes the eyes of faith to see that when the answer to your prayers is no, whatever happened was still in divine order.

The statement "In everything God works for good with those who love him" (Romans 8:28) is easier to understand if you realize that God *keeps* on working for good even though you may not yet see how. Jane can see how this occurred with her own misfortunes.

She could have said, "Poor me. I was burned, I had cancer, I had to move when I didn't want to, and I got a divorce. My life is a wreck and it's God's fault." Instead she looks back and says, "Because of these misfortunes I was able to do a lot of good things."

We were impressed to hear how psychiatrist Gerald Jampolsky helps to prepare terminally ill children and their families for impending death. The overriding feeling at the Center of Attitudinal Healing in Tiburon, California, he told us, is unconditional love. "People feel free to cry and go through their pain, as well as experience joy with each other. We introduce the thought that there is another way of looking at life and death; and that life and love being one and the same, they can be viewed as eternal and never-ending." Jampolsky added, "At our center, children help each other by talking about their fears of death with each other."

Many people who have lost a child know that such a loss is devastating. Yet they can see that in their ability to support and help others, good has come out of it. We believe that such people walk the same path as did Jesus, who died so that others could live.

Take a few moments right now to write in your notebook the tragic things that have happened to you. Then write how you have grown in this experience. You might write, "Because I got a divorce, I was motivated to get some counseling that helped me change for the better," or "When I lost my job, I had to learn some new skills to get another one, and these new skills make my present work more pleasant." Write down how you are using these insights to help others, or how you will do so in the future.

Using the POWER Tools to Create a Relationship with God

To meet your need for creating a relationship with God, start with the First POWER Tool and accept yourself as you are. Know that you are created in God's image, and for that reason you are a good and worthy person. If, however, you feel that you are separate from God in some way—if you have failed to love yourself or your fellow man and you see that bad consequences have followed—acknowledge that fact. In prayer tell God that you want to move out of this separation. Then accept the power you already have to act differently.

Using the Second POWER Tool—obtaining information—may be as simple as reading the Bible. Commit yourself to read some of it every day. Take advantage of study groups, inspiring books, and Bible courses. Read books by thinkers and leaders whose ideas ignite your spirit. Ask people you admire for suggestions of their favorite books.

Jane had been going to church all her life when her minister announced that he was going to teach a Bethel Bible course. Those who wanted to enroll would have to commit to attending the Sunday evening class for three years, study about seven hours a week, and take tests. Jane thought the whole idea was so crazy that she went around telling everyone she wouldn't think of taking it.

On the Sunday that the class was to begin, the minister announced that one more student was needed to meet the minimum enrollment requirements but that he was planning to start the class anyway because he knew that someone would enroll. Jane said in a loud voice to the person sitting next to her, "It won't be me!" But that night, as she was cooking spaghetti for guests who were coming for supper, she had an unshakable urge to go to church. She took off her apron and told her husband, "I'll just be a few minutes. I want to tell them I'm not going to take the Bethel course." She didn't return until 10 P.M.—after her husband had fed the dinner guests himself.

"When I got to the class, I realized that I had an innate hunger for studying the Bible. This desire had been working on me, but I had been resisting it," she said. She has been forever thankful that she signed up for the course. She learned how to "think Hebrew" so that the Old Testament battles and tribal customs became meaningful to her. She studied each book of the Bible, and after the course was over, she could no longer say, "There is no God." She had an irreversible belief.

While nothing can take the place of the Bible, we like to read other Christian books and inspiring literature, too. We particularly like C. S. Lewis's books. Go to a Christian bookstore and browse until you find something that appeals to you. Even better, ask God to lead you to the right books before you go to the store. You will be surprised at what you find.

The Golden Bridge Technique

Using the Third POWER Tool to meet this need involves learning how to pray more effectively. Most people know how to express their desires in prayer or contemplation, but few know how to rest while in God's presence and listen for the still, small voice within. This is the kind of quiet awareness that makes change possible for you.

Dr. Donald Curtis, author of *Your Thoughts Can Change Your Life*, suggests a way to combine visualizations with morning prayer, a technique that we have come to value. Visualize the day to come as a golden bridge in front of you leading to all the events you have scheduled. Then ask Christ to go with you across the bridge. See him walking with you as you meet a business client, relate to a difficult child, or have lunch with someone.

Throughout the day, as these scheduled events happen, you will feel a loving spirit extending to others through you. You can reach out in ways you never believed were possible.

Then, before you go to bed, rest once again in God's presence and go back over your day. See the times you failed to act as you truly wanted to. Change the unkind word you said. Visualize yourself having acted as you hoped to but didn't. See yourself being kinder and scheduling time more wisely. When you have made your day perfect, give thanks for it and go to sleep. This visualization is important because it enables you to rest rather than toss and turn. Also, when you use this exercise to correct your behavior before you go to sleep, you are programming your unconscious to help you act as you wish the next day, and the next.

Risking Your Way to Faith

If you haven't had a relationship with God, believing in him may seem like a tall order. "How can I believe something I really don't believe?" you may ask.

If you find that you know a lot *about* God but still don't feel one *with* him, you may wonder how to go about increasing your faith.

The Fourth POWER Tool, risking, is the answer. Risk doing the things that will build your faith. Set aside time every day to read the Bible and other inspiring material and to pray.

In Alcoholics Anonymous, thousands of people who had no belief have risked depending on a higher power to attain sobriety. Those who have been agnostics are often advised to think of their higher power as the group or as a rock or as their hip pocket. The strange thing is that when they risk believing that the group or the rock or the hip pocket will keep them from drinking, they find the strength to keep sober. Learning that there truly is a power that is greater than themselves, they are able to "let go and let God" make many changes in their lives. We believe that God so wants to help you that he will accept even the tiniest little bit of faith and give you good things.

Risk visiting churches until you find one that you feel comfortable in. Fill yourself with the beauty and wonder of worship services, and become energized by the friendship and faith of those around you.

Jane is grateful for having grown up in Winston-Salem, North Carolina, where she could attend the famous Moravian Easter sunrise service each year. Thousands of visitors come to Winston-Salem for that very purpose. Before daylight, five hundred members of brass bands echo hymns from different points of the city. Everyone converges on Salem Square in the dark to listen to the almost mystical-sounding music. When the church bell tolls at 6 A.M., the bishop appears and calls out, "The Lord is risen." The crowd cries back, "The Lord is risen, indeed." Then in total silence, all walk to God's Acre, an ancient cemetery where all the graves are covered with flowers. Even the oldest graves, some of which date back three hundred years, bear forsythia, jonquils, tulips, or azaleas—whatever is blooming at the season. Everyone stands and watches the sun come up over a hill covered with ancient cedar trees that were brought with the original Moravian settlers from Germany. In the awesome silence, with the beauty of the flowers all around, it is as if the living are united with those no longer on earth. "You cannot fail to believe in the resurrection when you are in the midst of all this majesty and beauty," says Jane. "The worship service itself is a resurrection."

Reaching Out to Build Faith

The more you use the Fifth POWER Tool and reach out to help others build their faith, the more your own faith will increase. When Jane was elected Miss Winston-Salem, her mother had a serious talk with her. "Jane, every time that you do something for the glory of Jane, do something for the glory of God," she said. "But don't go around talking about it," she warned, "because if you do, you will get your glory here on earth." Being a typical eighteen-year-old, Jane didn't want to do that, but her mother insisted. She helped Jane find things she could feel comfortable doing, such as visiting a nursing home or shut-ins or children in hospitals, or reading to the blind.

"Memories of all the parades I rode in and the honors I received that year have all faded, but I still remember the dear wrinkled hands that held onto mine and the trust in the children's faces," Jane says. She learned that reaching out has its own rewards, and yet she did receive a reward on earth, too. The Winston-Salem Board of Aldermen did something they had never done for any other Miss Winston-Salem. They surprised her with a special "Jane Carter Day" and proclaimed before the city council that Jane had exemplified loving qualities that truly made her a queen.

The Fullness of Time for You

Before Jane took the Bethel Bible course, she did not understand what other Christians meant when they used the Biblical term *the fullness of time* to describe when

Christ came to earth. (Ephesians 1:10). Then she learned that because of the Roman Empire, there was relative peace in the known world when Jesus was born. Rather than many official languages, there was only one. It was the time that God planned for Jesus to appear and to be made known to many. Jesus came at the only time in history when it would have been possible for Christianity to take hold. The promise is that everything in heaven and earth will be united with God through him.

We believe that there is a fullness of time for every person, as well. Just as Jesus was born two thousand years ago at a specific time, there is a fullness of time for you, too. Is the time now? We sincerely hope it is.

13

Healing Your Relationships —The Ninth Human Need

Like most brides and grooms, we were so excited and thrilled during our wedding that we couldn't concentrate on what our minister was saying. Only later, when we played the video tape of the ceremony, did we fully grasp the meaning of the poem she read from Kahlil Gibran's *The Prophet*.

"Let there be spaces in your togetherness, and let the winds of the heavens dance between you," she quoted, and then later on, "Give your hearts, but not into each other's keeping. For only the hand of Life can contain your hearts. And stand together yet not too near together: For the pillars of the temple stand apart, and the oak tree and the cypress grow not in each other's shadow."

Even in the closest of relationships, Gibran seems to be saying, you should not seek complete togetherness. You have to allow the other person to be different, to grow at a different rate from yourself, even at times to cause you discomfort. In other words, you have to work—sometimes very hard—to have a healthy relationship. We agree that this is true not only for man and wife, but for people in any kind of relationship.

You may be thinking, "I am accountable to no one but myself." But you *are* connected to everyone else! Carl Hammerschlag, the doctor we mentioned in chapter 11, who learned new ways of healing from the Indians, has wisely pointed out that belly buttons are a permanent reminder that we were once significantly connected with another human being—our mother. You can't escape your connectedness to other people. If you try to ignore it, the result will be that you have *unhealthy* relationships.

That is why we believe that the ability to work out good relationships between love partners, family members, and friends is a basic human need. The only insurance against being stuck in relationship tragedies is to care enough not only to learn to *relate* to others, but to *elate* them. How do you do that? Put God and spirit first. You will then find a special kind of joy and pride in yourself that radiates to the one you love.

A Three-Step Formula for Happiness

We define a healthy relationship as two or more people who have unconditional love for each other. That means that they are mutually committed to help each other be all that they can be; that they share feelings honestly and accept the other person, even when he or she is less than perfect. In unhealthy relationships, partners are committed to fulfilling their own needs rather than to helping each other.

Jane has experienced both kinds of relationships with the opposite sex. "Before I met Bob, a relationship with a man meant pain, high anxiety, and a search for approval. I thought that if I told a man what I really felt, he might get angry or, even worse, he might leave. Yes, there were some good moments, but underneath was a tone of fear, pain, and hurt."

Since we have been together, Jane doesn't feel that way any more. "While choosing the right partner was important, the biggest difference was in myself. I needed to understand that no other living human being could fill me with love. I had to come from a place of fullness that spilled over, and that meant finding what we call 'elation,'" Jane says.

Spiritual growth was the key. Once she had that realization, did she have to keep on working to maintain a healthy relationship? "Yes, and I always will, but now the effort is more like painting a beautiful picture instead of breaking my back digging a ditch. There's something glorious about it," she says.

How does a person find this fullness that Jane talks about? Before we were married, we had the pleasure of meeting John Paul Zahody, who wrote a short but powerful book titled *The Secret of Staying Together*. When we asked him what we could do to keep our relationship loving and supportive, he told us what he said in the book: The first step is *personal integrity*. "You must first become aware of the image of your ideal before you can express it in the activity of your lives," he told us. "Your ability to recognize the integrity of true commitment in yourself and in your partner comes directly from your own daily practice of integrity—from the quality of commitment to honesty, fairness, consistency, and excellence of performance that prevails in your personal affairs."

We gave Zahody's advice a lot of thought and devised

this simple, three-step formula for developing integrity and commitment:

1. Build a personal relationship with your spiritual self and with God. Work to feel that deep peacefulness each day (see chapter 12).

2. Love yourself. Feel beautiful from the inside out (see chapter 5).

3. Practice the Golden Rule. Whatever you would have the people with whom you are in relationship do to you, do also to them.

When you hear your "small, still voice" through daily prayer and meditation, you recognize that integrity means being honest, fair, and consistent, and you have God's help to live that way. When you give yourself permission to love yourself, you can express your own needs while allowing the other person to express his or hers. You don't ask the other person to deny personal needs in order to give you the love you should be giving yourself. When you practice the Golden Rule, you can accept the differences in your partner and love him or her unconditionally.

"In the past," Jane remembers, "I always said whatever I thought a man wanted to hear, regardless of the way I felt. Rather than love myself enough to take a risk in my relationship and work to help it grow, I told a lot of half-truths. Then I felt frustrated because I wasn't getting my way. The really strange thing was that the other person always perceived that I wasn't telling the whole truth, and that made him angry, too. I learned that when I expressed my honest feelings to the people who loved me, they felt special, needed, and closer to me—*if I also expressed a willingness to listen to their feelings*. Even when we continued to think differently, we allowed each other to maintain our own integrity.

"As Gibran said, we needed spaces between us through which the winds of heaven could dance. Instead, I tried to fill my need to be loved by manipulating others to love me. I didn't believe that it was possible to be true to myself, communicate the truth, and still find love," Jane says. "Now I know that love can flourish *only* where there is complete truthfulness."

Relationships are stronger when *both* partners have personal integrity and commitment. When you are seeking a relationship with the opposite sex, a friend, or a business associate, choose wisely. Though you may not have complete control over selecting family members or a business associate, you can improve even a poor relationship by loving God and yourself and practicing the Golden Rule. No matter what happens then, you will feel a sense of peace and confidence as you go along your way.

What Are Your Chances for Happiness with Others?

Are you a good prospect for having healthy relationships? Write in your notebook your answers to the following questions.

1. *What factors do you consider* when you select a love partner, a friend, or a business associate? Is physical attractiveness more important than integrity? Is financial success a necessity? Are you attracted to the other person largely because of his or her interest in you?

If you answered yes to the last three questions, you

are depending on others to meet your needs rather than meeting them yourself and then letting your confidence and self-worth spill out in the form of love and elation to another. If you regard physical attractiveness as essential, ask yourself how you feel about your own appearance. Do you need to improve the way you look? Or do you need to feel more worthy so that you can accept yourself as you are?

If money is your main criterion for selecting a partner or friend, consider whether you are looking to another to give you security. What else besides money can make you feel secure? What is it that you truly want?

If you don't feel strongly attracted to another person but go along with the relationship just because that person is attracted to you, ask yourself why you don't value yourself enough to look for someone you could enjoy more. Do you need to improve your self-image?

Letting yourself get involved in a relationship because you feel needy is a sure way to get yourself in trouble. First of all, another person cannot fill your needs for you. That becomes apparent as a relationship continues over a period of time. When you try to change the other person so that he or she *can* fill your needs, you quickly discover it is impossible. Then you are stuck in disappointment, anger, and frustration. If you detect that you are seeking relationships because of your own neediness, work on meeting your own needs first. Then you will have something to give to the relationship that will improve it.

Write out some strengths you have that could be used to improve a relationship. For instance, you might write, "I have a good sense of humor," or "I care enough about myself to do aerobic exercise," or "I am learning how to have a positive mental attitude." If you have not met the ten basic needs we have listed in this book, write goals to work on them.

2. *Is honesty important to you?* Are you able to see the truth in a situation even when that truth is not to your liking? Can you allow another person to be honest with you?

Honesty not only means being truthful and refusing to steal or cheat; it also means being able to look at a disagreement between yourself and another and opt to do *what* is right rather than focus on *who* is right. A couple whom we'll call Dan and Eve had money problems because they weren't being entirely honest with each other. Both financially independent before they married, they agreed to maintain separate bank accounts. This worked fine until the water heater broke. Then each expected the other to pay the plumber. Neither did. As the plumber's calls became more insistent, Dan's and Eve's resentment of each other grew. They were almost on the point of separating. Finally, in desperation they sat down and communicated their feelings honestly. Dan recently had paid for some new furniture, and he thought he deserved to use his current income to make payments on a sports car. Eve paid many of the grocery bills, and she felt she deserved to buy the designer dresses she wanted. Who was right? Dan and Eve valued their relationship enough to be honest about *what* was right rather than to argue about *who* was right. They decided to set up a budget that included household expenses like plumbing bills, to which both would contribute an equal percentage of their income.

Think of a disagreement you have had in a relationship, and consider it honestly. Write down the solution that demonstrates *what* is right rather than *who* is right.

3. *Can you communicate fairly?* Do you consider the other person's feelings when you are expressing your own? Do you know how to listen?

When Bob was a sophomore in high school, he went out one night with a senior who persuaded him to get drunk. After passing out in front of the youth center, Bob was taken to jail. His parents, who didn't drink at all, were mortified and angry that they had to go to the jail at 2 A.M. to bail out their son. They could have communicated their feelings with judgmental "you" statements. They could have said, "You are a no-good son who will never amount to anything," but they didn't. The next morning, as Bob nursed a headache, his father used "I" statements to express his disapproval of Bob's *actions* rather than of him as a *person*. He told him, "I was disappointed that you got drunk. I was really ashamed to find you in jail." Then he added his reassurance of unconditional love: "I want you to know that I still love you."

Bob will be forever grateful that his father did not verbally abuse him for a mistake he was already ashamed of.

Another communication tool that demonstrates unconditional love is listening. Every evening we ask each other how our day has been. Then, without interrupting, criticizing, or giving advice, we take time to listen to all the frustrations and the successes. We do this not only because we love each other and are interested in each other, but because we know that each of us need to talk about our day. This is one way that we nurtu each other and our marriage relationship.

Think of how another person caused you disapp ment and hurt. Write how you feel about the situ using "I" statements. Then express your love person who was responsible. For instance, let's you and your husband attend a party and the conversation turns to politics. When you express your opinion, your husband says, "Oh, don't listen to her, she never reads the paper, and she's completely ignorant about the issues." Even though you are smouldering, you say nothing because you don't want to make a scene. In your notebook you might write, "I get angry when my husband puts me down in front of others. I am disappointed that I did not express my feelings about being put down. I love my husband enough to tell him how I feel and to ask him not to put me down in the future. I accept the fact that just as I am not perfect, my husband is not perfect, either. I love my husband and forgive him."

4. *Do you know yourself well enough to recognize the unstated personal boundaries you have set up that you "expect" others never to cross?* Are you able to communicate about your boundaries?

Lots of people build emotional walls to defend preferences they are determined to keep secret. We know secretaries who go out of their way to please their boss by typing the most intricate reports but draw the line at sharpening pencils . . . men who don't like women who wear black . . . and parents who "expect" their children to be quiet on Saturday mornings while they sleep in. But do they verbalize their expectations? No!

It's all right to have boundaries for others, but if they are important to you, then do tell people about them. Otherwise, the secretary who won't sharpen pencils will find her boss giving her a bad performance review. The man who doesn't like black will likely sulk when his girlfriend appears for an important date in a new black dress that she adores. The parents who want to sleep in Saturday mornings will find themselves yelling at their children to turn down the TV and unable to sleep because they are too angry.

If you cannot define your boundaries for others, ask yourself if you secretly fear losing the relationship by stating your preferences. Are you afraid that you are not worthy of having boundaries? If so, go back and fulfill your need to be beautiful on the inside.

It is a good idea to have healthy boundaries for yourself. For example, it is important to establish a limit on how far you will go in expressing anger during an argument. If you have created a boundary for yourself that says, "I refuse to express my anger in hurtful ways," you can avoid making vicious, unfair statements that destroy relationships.

Write down some boundaries you have set up for those with whom you are in a relationship. Do they know about these boundaries? If not, write how you would tell them, using "I" statements to express your feelings. Now write down the boundaries you have set for yourself.

For example, let's say that in your family, people didn't make a big deal about giving expensive presents for birthdays. No one seemed to mind. Your wife, however, keeps giving you expensive presents that break the budget. When you give her a token present, she looks hurt. You might write in your notebook, "I have a boundary against spending money to try to prove that we love each other. I will tell her that and say that if she wants to express love for me, then I would rather she do it by making my favorite supper rather than by spending a lot of money. I will make a special effort to express my love to her on her birthday, and I will set a boundary on myself against getting angry and complaining if my wife does buy me an expensive present."

Or perhaps your husband has smoked for years and

you have put up with the fumes all this time without saying a word, because you have put a boundary on expressing your real feelings to your husband when you disagree with him. You might write in your notebook, "I will tell him, 'The smoke from your cigarettes really bothers my sinuses, and besides, it permeates our whole house. I'd like for you to go outside when you smoke.' At the same time, I will set a boundary on myself not to nag him about smoking."

5. *Are you secure enough to allow others in a relationship to be different from you?* Do you expect the other person to achieve what you haven't been able to achieve?

When Kahlil Gibran wrote about allowing spaces between togetherness through which the wind could blow, he was talking about the need to accept the differences in others. Parents, especially, seem to have a problem with this requirement. How many fathers have you seen on the Little League field, screaming at a son because either he doesn't play ball as well as Dad did when he was young or doesn't play ball *better* than Dad did? It is hard to accept differences in your children's personality or physique if your own self-image is insecure. If you were a good ball player, be glad that you excelled in a sport and help your son find *something else* for which he has a natural aptitude that can be developed. If you were not a good ball player yourself, recognize that it was okay that you weren't and that you have other talents. Then accept the fact that you are beautiful on the inside anyway, and give your son permission to be the special person he was meant to be, too.

Jane once taught an eighth-grader named Tim who had been placed in her honors class for gifted children. Tim's parents, who had only a high school education, were fiercely proud of Tim's high IQ. But Tim wanted to play, not study. When he made some D's and F's, Jane suggested that Tim be returned to the former class. But Tim's father was insulted. "You will do the work or I'll beat you to pieces," he threatened Tim. Between the father's pressure to work and Tim's inclination to play, Tim continued to make poor grades. When Tim received the next report card, he attempted to erase the D's and F's, and write in A's and B's. Jane discovered the changes and called the father in for a conference. The father bristled at her suggestions that he stop pressuring Tim.

"I know Tim is a gifted child. You're crazy if you think that I'm going to let him drop out of that class," he told her. Jane replied, "I know he is intelligent, but something is wrong. Either Tim is afraid of failure or of you." Tim's father could not see that he was placing his own need to feel successful on his unwilling son. Tim remained in the honors class and limped through the school year. The next year when he went to high school, his first report card showed two D's and an F. Before he let his father see it, Tim put a shotgun in his mouth and pulled the trigger. He was dead at fourteen because he couldn't live up to the expectations his father had forced on him.

What is the difference between setting standards for children and pressuring them too much? After teaching for many years, Jane believes that most parents need a lighter touch. Somehow, when a parent first holds his or her new baby, the overriding emotion seems to be "I have to do everything right. I want my child to grow up perfect. And I don't want him to make the same mistakes I made." Having a sense of responsibility is good. But some parents, because of a poor self-image, fail to balance this loving desire with loving realism.

Who can achieve perfection? Are you a failure if your child doesn't excel at everything? We believe that most parents could do a better job of developing the unique gifts God gave their children by lightening up on the responsibilities and putting more time into loving them and having fun with them.

Our veterinarian recently gave us advice on dog training when we bought Sunny, our new puppy. He said, "Always scratch dogs under the chin so that they will look at you. Don't say no so often that they become timid and afraid. And always praise them lavishly for the things they do right." We think that's excellent child-rearing advice, too!

We also like what Kahil Gibran wrote about children: "You may give them your love, but not your thoughts, for they have their own thoughts. You may house their bodies, but not their souls, for their souls dwell in the house of tomorrow, which you cannot visit, not even in your dreams."

If you have children, describe the ways in which they are different from you that irritate you. Affirm the positive aspects of their differences. Then tell them what you appreciate about them.

Giving Forth Instead of Giving Up

We have saved the most important question for last. Here it is: *When someone in a relationship disappoints you or does something to harm you, are you able to forgive that person?* When you are in a close relationship, inevitably there will be times when you are hurt, disappointed, and misunderstood. You may feel that it is impossible to mend a relationship once trust has been broken. Or you may be able to tell the other person that you forgive him or her, but still harbor negative feelings. That is not forgiving. To us, forgiving means "giving forth," not holding onto painful memories. It means wiping the slate clean, as if the hurtful actions had never happened.

How do you forgive in this way? If you know that you are beautiful on the inside in spite of the ways in which you have hurt others, you can better accept disappointments that others bring because at the very core of yourself, you know you cannot be diminished. Try looking at the situation from your partner's viewpoint. Take a step back and look at your entire relationship, and see the other things that are good about it.

Bob and his former wife, Cindy, have asked for forgiveness from each other for their divorce and assured each other that they have forgiven. They act on their forgiveness, too. They sometimes talk to each other on the telephone. They freely share their thoughts and even ask each other for advice. Jane considers Cindy a friend. When Cindy comes to Dallas, Jane often has lunch with her.

Bob says, "When Cindy asked me to forgive her for not understanding the problems in our marriage, I told her, 'There's nothing to forgive. You were doing the best you could do at that time in your life. When I look at our relationship, I see that ninety-five percent of what we had was good and healthy. I don't have any regrets about our relationship.'"

Jane says, "Bob and Cindy could each have blamed the other for wrecking their marriage, but they didn't. Neither did they say, 'Please forgive me, but if you hadn't done such and such, it wouldn't have happened.' They totally released anything that could have thrown up a wall between them."

How many times should we forgive someone who does us wrong? Jesus told his disciples to forgive seventy times seven times (Matthew 18:22), and he set the example. When Peter swore to Jesus that he would always be faithful to him, Jesus told Peter that he would deny him three times on the night of his betrayal. Even though Peter wanted to be faithful, his fear caused him to do the very thing that Jesus predicted. He denied that he was Jesus' disciple. He even denied knowing him! Yet Jesus forgave Peter. He forgave him so entirely that he trusted him to lead the other disciples to form the Christian church.

Is there anyone whom you need to forgive? If so, describe the disagreement as if you were the other person writing about it. Is there anything you did that contributed to the problem? If so, write it down. Now write down all the good things about your relationship. Do you want to maintain the relationship? If so, what can you do to make it better?

Bob used this technique when he discovered that Jane had not told him about two large debts she had incurred before they were married. Disappointed, he told himself that we had agreed to tell each other exactly what our financial situation was, and that she had lied to him. The issue seemed to be a lack of trust. When he wrote the situation from Jane's viewpoint, however, he saw that his businesslike approach had frightened Jane. She feared that if she admitted she had spent so much money in a way that he wouldn't approve, he would be angry. He wrote down, "I love Jane dearly and want to maintain the relationship. Therefore I will tell her that I am disappointed that she lied to me, but that I forgive her and will say no more about her debts. I want her to know that I am not going to 'punish' her if I am disappointed in the future. From now on, I will try to make it easier for her to come to me when she has a problem." Such communication allows us to have a more trusting relationship.

Using the POWER Tools to Improve Your Relationships

As you can tell by writing your answers to the above questions, it can be difficult to get an accurate picture of yourself in relation to others. Pride, feelings of insecurity, and a poor self-image get in the way. You can use the First POWER Tool to see yourself as you really are, a person of great worth who nevertheless may need to make some changes. If you are convinced you made a mistake in choosing the wrong partner, admit it. Then set goals to develop a healthier relationship. If you see that you need to improve your communication skills or learn how to forgive, resolve to make those improvements.

The Second POWER Tool, obtaining information to make changes, leads you to helpful books, counseling sources, and support groups. For couple relationships, we find John Paul Zahody's *The Secret of Staying Together* and John Powell's *The Secret of Staying in Love* especially helpful. Marriage encounter groups are a great way to learn to communicate more meaningfully with your partner. For parents, *Parent Effectiveness Training* by Dr. Thomas Gordon teaches how to communicate with children—or anyone else.

Pink Bubbles and Prayer Togetherness

You can use the Third POWER Tool's techniques of visualization and affirmation to make your efforts toward building good relationships more effective. One that we especially like is the pink bubble visualization, which we learned from Shakti Gawain's *Creative Vis-*

ualization. While you are visualizing or praying, simply see your relationship as you would really like it to be. For instance, if your son seems rebellious, picture yourself doing something with him that you both enjoy. Then see him looking at you with love in his eyes. Surround this visualization with a beautiful bubble that is pink, the color of the heart. Then release the bubble. See it float off into space as you affirm that God wants you to have a good relationship with your child. In this way you are able to let go of the negative feelings you have about your son. You are open to the manifestation of a good relationship between you.

Jane used the pink bubble visualization when we started dating. Then we broke up. Had God failed her? Not at all. He was manifesting our need to bring a spiritual element into our relationship.

Now we know that praying together is necessary for us to maintain a healthy relationship. When we have disagreements and are feeling impatient or frustrated, we tell God in front of the other person how we are feeling. Then we ask him to grant us the ability to be more loving, forgiving, and patient.

Bob explains, "It's difficult sometimes to look at Jane and say, 'I'm sorry,' or 'Forgive me for being impatient.' It's easier to tell God about it. When Jane hears me ask for help to be more understanding and accepting, our relationship is strengthened."

No Pain, No Gain

The Fourth POWER Tool encourages you to risk new behavior in your relationship. Do you have the courage to tell others the boundaries you have set for them? To communicate your feelings in "I" statements? To forgive?

Sometimes it seems simpler just to ignore misunderstandings or little hurts that evolve in a relationship. Don't! As athletes are fond of saying when their muscles ache because they have pushed themselves to run an extra mile or lift a heavier weight, "No pain, no gain." The rewards of risking new behavior are worth it.

The Fifth POWER Tool encourages you to start reaching out to others with simple steps. Demonstrate your desire for a good relationship by making phone calls, writing notes, and giving praise. Also use this tool to reach out to people who don't have a good relationship. Tell them the things you have learned to do that will help them to nurture their own relationships.

Be ... Do ... Have

A young woman, her face taut with pain and anger, stood at the back of one of Jane's human development seminars. "My kids are driving me crazy," she confessed during a sharing session. "I have a two-year-old who refuses to be potty-trained, a six-year-old having trouble learning to read, and an eight-year-old who has so many problems I can't describe them all. I'm so tired! I can't even go to the bathroom without being pestered by those kids."

Jane asked her, "What is really true about what you have just said?"

The woman replied, "I *should* be able to get things done and be sure that the kids get everything they need. I try hard, *but* I just don't have time for three kids. They're driving me crazy! *If only* my husband would help!"

As the woman talked, Jane spotted clues to the reason for her problems. This woman talked of "shoulds" and "oughts" and "buts." She kept saying, "*If only* things were different." The more Jane asked her what was true about the situation, the more she sounded like a victim of circumstances beyond her control.

When Jane pressed her again and again to say what was true, the woman finally admitted, with tears rolling down her cheeks, "I don't want to be a mother." Because she feared criticism, she had not even been able to think this incriminating thought. But Jane assured her that the truth of a situation is never right or wrong or good or bad, it just *is*.

"Just allow it to be, no matter what it is," she said. "Remember that Jesus said, 'The truth shall make you free.'" Then she went on to explain that human beings have choices. If they are stuck in a bad situation, they don't have to stay stuck. The woman immediately began to identify some things she could do. First she was going to tell her husband that she was frustrated and needed his help. Second, she would hire a teen-aged girl to do some minor housework, allowing herself more time to enjoy her children. Finally, she promised to sign up for a Parent Effectiveness Training class to learn the communication skills she needed in order to express herself to her husband and children.

Because this young woman was willing to accept herself as she was and to choose to change, she is now a different person. She often finds it exciting to be a mother. Her relationship with her husband and her children is excellent.

This mother did what we hope you will do: Love God and yourself, and practice the Golden Rule to meet your need for having healthy relationships. If you do, you will find that other people bring joy and meaning— and yes, even elation—to your life.

14

Getting and Giving Love —The Tenth Human Need

One evening Jane was on a plane returning home after conducting a seminar. After an exhausting schedule, she looked forward to spending three relaxing hours in the air. The flight didn't exactly work out that way. Shortly after the plane was airborne, the captain's voice came over the speaker. "Please keep your seat belts on. We are approaching a thunderstorm. We plan to fly around it, but we will be experiencing some turbulence," he said.

He wasn't fooling. The plane started bouncing up and down like a paddleball on a string. Drinks slid around on the serving trays while the passenger next to Jane gave up his supper to a paper sack. Jane felt a prickle of fear.

When the captain advised everyone to fold up their trays and put their drinks on the floor, she knew the situation was serious. With a sickening lurch, the plane dropped as if it were being sucked down by a huge vacuum cleaner. Inside the cabin, oxygen masks popped out of their overhead compartments. Pandemonium broke out. People screamed and cried and called for the flight attendants. No one knew what to do.

"Every time you ride a plane you are told how to use the oxygen masks, but evidently no one listens. I was as terrified as everyone else. I couldn't push back the chilling thought 'We're not going to make it.' I began to cry," Jane remembers.

"As we struggled with the masks, the captain told us that we had been caught in a downdraft and had lost altitude. We were flying at nine thousand feet, which is not nearly high enough for a big jet airliner. Every time the plane shuddered and groaned, people screamed. We all expected to crash any minute.

"Wild thoughts flashed through my mind. 'I'm not ready to die! I have so much that I still want to do. What about all the people I care about? I've never told them I love them!' I kept thinking.

"Eventually, however, the plane did land safely. We all staggered into the airport on shaky legs and made a dash for the telephones. Right then and there I called everyone I could think of and told them, 'I'm sorry I never told you this before, but I want you to know that I love you.'"

It may have been the hard way to learn it, but Jane had discovered what many people do not know. Each of us has a need to give and receive love.

In fact, the need for love is the most important of all the ten basic human needs we have explored in this book. You can live (or perhaps we should say exist) without self-esteem, a positive mental attitude, productivity, self-discipline, an awareness of beauty, and humor. You can even live without having physical health, a personal relationship with God, and good relationships with others. True, you cannot reach the goal of self-actualization without meeting these needs. You may feel badly stuck, but you keep on living. Without love, however, you die.

This life-or-death need for love was discovered after World War II in several British foundling homes. So many parents had died in the blitz that these foundling homes were full of orphaned infants. Attendants gave them the best of care. They fed them nutritionally balanced formulas, kept them dry and clean, and made sure that they were warm and comfortable. For some unexplained reason, however, many infants who were born healthy sickened and died.

Then a group of nuns started going into one of the homes to hold the babies at other times besides when they were being fed or diapered. The nuns rocked them, talked and sang to them, and cuddled them, much as a mother would do. The death rate in this home dropped radically. The nursing staff wondered, could it be that the babies had died because they weren't being touched, cuddled, and loved? When scientists researched this theory, they found it to be true. The babies were dying of *marasmus*. Their bodies, deprived of the sensations of love, could not assimilate the proteins and calories in their food. They were literally dying of starvation for love, even though their formulas contained everything their bodies needed.

In adults, the lack of love does not cause *physical* death. Instead, loneliness, apathy, depression, and an inability to function as you would like are some of the results. According to psychologists Carin Rubenstein and Phillip Shaver, authors of *In Search of Intimacy*, one-quarter of American people say they are lonely. Millions escape the resulting pain through mind-changing chemicals, overeating, overwork, gambling, and other addictions. Millions more have feelings of apathy and fatigue, as well as chronic aches and pains. Without love, the death you experience is mental, emotional, and spiritual.

Love as we define it, however, means more than *receiving* the care and concern of others. It also means *giving* of yourself to others. When you do both, you develop joy and find strength even when life presents you with a challenge. You can achieve far more than you ever thought possible.

The Extraordinary Thing About Love

Jane's father once heard a group of coaches talking about how love transformed a Columbia University fourth-string running back into a star back in the fifties. The young man involved was a senior who had been on the playing field only twice during his four years on the team. Just before an important game, he telephoned his coach.

"Coach, I won't be able to practice this week. You see, my dad just died and I need permission to go home," he said. The coach expressed his condolences and told him not to worry about Saturday's game. "Just be there for your family," he said.

On Friday, however, the young man telephoned him again. "Coach, I've decided I have to come back to play tomorrow."

"Son, you don't have to do that. Your family needs you. Don't even think about the game," the coach told him. But the young man insisted. On Saturday he was all suited up. Futhermore, he begged the coach to put him in the starting lineup.

"But you've never started in a football game," the coach protested.

"I know, but you've just got to start me today," he

insisted. The coach wasn't sure why he agreed to do so, but he did, warning that he would pull him out the minute he did anything to hurt the team. That day, the young man ran four touchdowns before the half, leading to an impressive win. The coach didn't know whether to kiss or kick the young man.

"You never told me you could play football like that! What have you been waiting for?" he demanded.

Then the young man said, "Coach, my dad was blind. And today was the first day he ever saw me play football." His love for his father had given him coordination, strength, and power that he had never had before.

The Four Faces of Love

Since each person must work out his or her own way of giving and receiving love, the definitions of love are many. St. Paul described it this way: "Love is patient and kind; love is not jealous or boastful; it is not arrogant or rude. Love does not insist on its own way; it is not irritable or resentful; it does not rejoice at wrong, but rejoices in the right. Love bears all things, believes all things, hopes all things, endures all things" (I Corinthians 13).

When Bob took a college course in marriage and the family, he defined love as "an unselfish giving of one person to the other without expecting anything in return." He still thinks that that is a good definition. "Love is valuing what is precious and good and Godlike in ourselves and in our friends, family, and mates, and responding to that value with care, concern, and intimacy," he says.

The Greek language has several words to describe different kinds of love. *Eros* describes romantic love, which may involve physical intimacy. It is that blissful feeling of falling in love that leads you to commit yourself to another. It is also the form of love that leads to the procreation of the human race. Jane says it is like "going ga-ga" over someone, because it is so totally irrational. When you are in *eros*, you are like an infant who adores its parents because they fulfill all its needs. Because no one can do for you what you must do for yourself, however, *eros* cannot last. The excitement inevitably lessens, and unless it is replaced by a more mature form of love, the relationship dies. In fact, you may be smitten with *eros* for a partner who is totally unsuited to you. Even so, you have the choice of rejecting such a relationship. We believe that *eros* is valuable only when it causes two people to commit themselves to grow into the kind of love that inspires them to want the best for each other.

Philia is the Greek word for the love of friends or of your fellow man. Fraternities often use this word to describe the special caring relationship they want their members to have for each other. American Indians practiced *philia* when they pledged loyalty as blood brothers. In everyday life, you have *philia* when you revere a friendship, delight in another's presence, and do everything you can to make life better for that person.

When Leo Buscaglia offered his now famous Love 101 course, students vied to get a seat in his classroom. Buscaglia's advice to hug others turned into a revolution that now has people all over the United States demonstrating *philia* with their arms. We believe that hugging is a marvelous way to begin experiencing love. When you hug, you are giving of yourself and allowing yourself to be vulnerable to others. Your touch tells others that they are valuable to you. Usually you receive love in return.

Agape love, according to Webster's, is "spontaneous self-giving love expressed freely without calculation of cost or gain to the giver or merit on the part of the receiver." Like God's love for you, *agape* is the highest form of love. It is easy to want the best for someone who in turn wants the best for you. When you are rejected, however, it is considerably harder to keep on reaching out to the other person. Yet that is what *agape* is all about. In our opinion, you have not experienced genuine love unless you have practiced *agape*.

Why is this true? As we saw in chapter 13, no human being is perfect. Unless you can give love spontaneously without calculating the cost, love for a romantic partner or your fellow human being will founder at the first disagreement.

Perhaps you've heard the statement "Those who need love the most deserve it the least." Jane learned this lesson in *agape* love from a teacher when she was in the fourth grade. She had started the year with a young teacher with beautiful flaming red hair whom she adored. Then, because of overcrowding, she and some other students were transferred to the classroom of Mrs. Reece, an older woman. Nothing was wrong with Mrs. Reece as a teacher, but Jane was angry at losing her beautiful young teacher. She refused to do her homework. She pouted and whispered about Mrs. Reece in class. She complained about her at home.

In April, Jane began to have a recurring pain in her left knee. Then one Sunday morning she could not stand up in church. After her doctor ran tests, he gave her parents the dreaded diagnosis—cancer. Jane received massive doses of chemotherapy. Lying in the hospital bed, ten-year-old Jane endured pain and weakness. Fortunately, something good happened to Jane. Every day Mrs. Reece came to tell her what was going on in

school and to teach her lessons. She read stories and
brought gifts and letters from the other children. She
talked to Jane about getting better and coming back to
school. When she saw discouragement on Jane's face,
she told Jane that she loved her and that she looked
forward to their time together every day.

Mrs. Reece never mentioned how spitefully Jane had
treated her in the classroom. Instead, the teacher demonstrated only her care and concern. To this day, whenever Jane thinks of someone who instilled hope and
positive thoughts, she remembers Mrs. Reece.

"We fell in love," she says. "The next year, when I
was well and in the fifth grade, I went by her room
every day just to visit."

Mrs. Reece was reaching out to Jane even though
Jane initially rejected Mrs. Reece. In the end, this *agape*
love helped Jane heal and commit herself to a role
model who demonstrated *agape*.

When we tried to have an *eros* relationship before
we were married, we could not maintain it. After we
broke up, we didn't even have *philia* love for each other.
Looking back, we understood why this happened when
we read the definition of love that F. Scott Peck gave
in his dynamic book *The Road Less Traveled*. Peck said
that love is the will to extend oneself for the purpose
of nurturing one's own or another's spiritual growth.
Our relationship succeeded when we made the choice
to do just that. After we decided to see each other again,
we both pledged to bring a spiritual dimension into our
relationship. We took action to demonstrate care and
concern for each other. We grew closer by learning to
pray together. We allowed each other to grow. Our
relationship became strong as we learned to practice
agape.

Inevitably, we discovered that in order to love in this

way, we needed *self-love*. As described in chapter 5, self-love is having a regard for your own happiness, being able to accept yourself as you truly are and nurturing yourself even when you make mistakes, telling yourself that you deserve to have good things in life. If you have not met your basic human need for feeling beautiful from the inside out, it will be hard for you to reach out to another with care, concern, and intimacy, because you cannot fill another's cup when your own is empty.

Jesus said, "You shall love your neighbor *as yourself*" (Matthew 22:39). How many people hear the admonition to love their neighbors but shut their ears entirely to the requirement to love themselves? If you are always putting yourself down and telling yourself that you are not worthy of love, you will have nothing to give to others. It will be equally difficult for you to receive the love they give to you.

We believe that you can develop the ability to love at the highest level if you follow the same rules we gave you to improve relationships:

1. First love God and know that he loves you.

2. Love yourself.

3. Follow the Golden Rule with those you love. In other words, *work* to develop *agape* love.

How Well Prepared Are You to Love Another?

Since the first step in developing genuine love for another is to love yourself, use the First POWER Tool to accept the fact that you are created in God's image. If

God is love, then you are a loving person. If you don't feel that you are, or if you feel that others do not love you, answer the following questions. They will help you determine what steps you can take to open yourself to *agape* love.

1. *Do you feel that your friends or your mate secretly would prefer a relationship with someone other than yourself?*

We know a man whose compulsive jealousy is threatening to destroy the genuine love that his beautiful wife has for him. Al accuses Teri of flirting with her male coworkers. If she arrives home later than usual, he insists on a minute-by-minute accounting of her time. The marriage and Teri's career are both suffering. Al cannot feel secure in his love because he is operating out of his own need and insecurity rather than a desire to care for Teri and help her to grow in her career so that her happiness enriches their union. To be able to practice *agape*, he must first work to improve his self-image.

We also know a woman named Elizabeth who has developed agoraphobia. While she is housebound, her husband must shop for groceries and drive car pools for the children after he comes home from work. His resentment is increasing every day. Why doesn't Elizabeth do something to help herself recover? She secretly believes that she is unlovable, so she ties her husband to her with her agoraphobia. She looks to him to fill all her emotional needs, and both she and her husband are miserable. Her dependency is standing in the way of *agape*.

If you secretly feel unlovable, write a goal in your notebook to develop your feeling of worthiness. (See chapter 5 for more help in meeting this need.) Think of ten good things about yourself and write them down. Affirm that God made you, that you have unique gifts, and that you deserve to be good to yourself.

2. *Do you feel that there are some secrets about yourself that you cannot reveal even to a close friend or a spouse?* Do you have fears, resentment, angers, or disappointments that you cannot share with those whose love you value?

If this is your feeling, you have a fear of intimacy. Like many men who feel that they must protect their masculine image at all costs, you may seem cold and uncaring. While it is wrong to expect the one you love to fulfill all your needs, it is right to share your humanness and let the other person see that you are not perfect. If your loved one does not know how you feel, how can he or she demonstrate the affection, care, and concern you crave? How can someone love you if you will not allow an opening in your heart for that person to enter?

From all appearances, Jerry had it made. By the age of twenty-seven, he was comptroller for a chain of stores. He had a kind and loving wife and a baby son. Jerry never told his wife about the times he felt insecure in his job. He stuffed down his fears and tried to maintain control. From his wife's viewpoint, however, Jerry seemed short-tempered and overly strict with their son. When she tried to talk to him about it, he became angry and self-protective. The marriage failed. When Jerry went to a divorce recovery workshop, he heard others expressing their real feelings. Some even cried. Then he saw what he had never seen before: When people revealed things about themselves which made them feel ashamed or disappointed or angry, other people comforted them. Jerry is now working on being able to share his feelings with those with whom he wants to be intimate. He believes that he will be a better marriage partner in the future.

If you have a fear of intimacy, set a goal of letting yourself be more vulnerable with persons you love. Write down all the things about yourself that you do not like. Then write some affirmations about yourself. Remember that you are a child of God who is not expected to be perfect but only to want to do the best you can. Then select three of the statements about yourself that you would be willing to share with the person to whom you are closest.

Let's say that you, like Jerry, feel that you're not doing as well at your job as you would like, and you are afraid you might even be fired. Resolve to admit to your wife that you just can't seem to relax and socialize with your coworkers as you should. If you have not been in the habit of sharing what you don't like about yourself, it may seem somewhat scary to tell your wife about these feelings.

This is a good time to use Emotional Transfusion (see chapter 11). Relax at alpha and enjoy the emotional glow from your donor visualization for five minutes. Then shift to the receiver visualization. Picture yourself telling your wife how you feel about your job, meanwhile transfusing positive feelings into the scene. See your wife listening with a sympathetic look on her face, then see her hug you. Do this several times and you will find that it is not so difficult to share your deepest thoughts with your partner.

3. *Do you believe that it would be a breach of love to end a relationship with a person who is destructive to you?* Do you feel most attracted to people who need your help?

If this is your problem, you and the one you love are both coming from a position of neediness. It means that you can only feel worthy if you are letting yourself be trampled. This is not love. It is an addiction.

Marti's son Rick didn't seem able to hold a job. He would work for a few months, then come home to sleep all day and hit the bars at night. Whenever he asked for money, Marti gave it to him, even though she was a widow who had barely enough for herself. "I can't bear to see him going without things," Marti explained. "If my love for him is strong enough, it will motivate him to change."

Rick's behavior was typical of those addicted to any mind-changing chemical. He depended on drinking and blaming others to escape his feelings of failure. But Marti was co-addicted. She blamed herself for Rick's failures and found solace and self-worth in sacrificing herself on the altar of guilt.

We know women and men who marry one addicted person after another, always insisting, "He needs me," or "I can help her." Alcohol isn't the only addiction. Sometimes it is gambling or overeating or sexual infidelity or abusiveness.

If this is your problem, write a goal to get professional help. Then compose a list of affirmations about yourself. Whenever you have thoughts that you must help a self-destructive person, affirm that you love yourself too much to destroy yourself. Recognize that it is ultimately more loving to let the self-destructive person reap the consequences of his or her mistakes so that he or she can realize that it is necessary to make changes.

4. *Do you feel that any kind of love is better than the alternative of having to spend time by yourself?*

Many people endure unhappy friendships and even

marriages simply because they are afraid to be alone. Patti had lots of friends, but she didn't really feel close to any of them. Yet whenever she found herself alone in her apartment, she telephoned the very people whose company she didn't enjoy. For hours she talked about things that bored her just to avoid being alone.

If your relationships are equally unsatisfactory, make it a goal to spend time developing your spiritual life when you are alone. Read books and listen to tapes that inspire and motivate you. Spend time in meditation and in prayer. As you listen to your inner voice and feel God's love for you, you will come to appreciate yourself and welcome solitude. Without knowing how it happens, you will feel better about yourself and more capable of making loving friendships.

Finding Information About How to Love

Using the Second POWER Tool, take advantage of the many sources of information designed to help you learn the right way to love. A favorite book of ours is the Bible, which is the story of God's unconditional love. We also like John Powell's *Staying in Love* and Leo Buscaglia's books.

Jane used to love to read Martin Bell's story of "Barrington Bunny" in *The Way of the Wolf* to her son Miles. While it sounded like a children's story, it was really a metaphor about *agape* love. Barrington was a lop-eared bunny with shiny eyes who was miserable on Christmas Eve because he had no one with whom to enjoy the festivities. He tried to attend the squirrels' party, but he couldn't climb a tree. He couldn't be with the beavers because he couldn't swim. The mice couldn't hear what he said because they were down in their holes. Finally he met a big silver wolf who asked what was wrong.

"I don't have any family and it is Christmas Eve," he sobbed.

"But, Barrington, every animal in the forest is your family," the wolf told him. Barrington was overjoyed. He began to take gifts to everyone. He collected fresh grass as a gift for the squirrels and left it in the tree with a note that said it was from "a member of your family." He gave sticks as a present to the beavers. Then, in the midst of a blizzard, he found a lost baby mouse, who he knew would surely die if he did not keep it warm. So Barrington tucked the mouse underneath his furry coat and shielded him from the bitter cold. All during the terrible night, he listened to the mouse's heartbeat. He realized that he had a wonderful gift to give to the mouse—the warmth of his fur and the shelter of his body. "All the animals in the forest are my friends," he told himself. The next morning the mouse's parents found their baby safe and sound beneath the frozen form of Barrington. All day Barrington's body lay there, while the big silver wolf stood guard over it.

Jane says, "In this simple story I could see the metaphor for true, unconditional love." Jesus loved in the same way.

Books are wonderful means of inspiration, and so are people who love you the way that Jesus did.

Techniques to Help You Love

Use the Third POWER Tool to ask God to help you become a more loving person. Pray together with the one you love. Ask God's help in forgiving each other when misunderstandings occur.

If a feeling of unworthiness is standing in the way of your giving love to others, you may want to use the good mother/good father meditation. It is especially effective for those who have come from an unhappy family or who did not feel loved as children. By using the meditation, you can become your own good parent who nurtures you now, freeing you from your feelings of unworthiness. Simply read this meditation into a tape recorder and play it back to yourself while you are in a relaxed, prayerful state. Or memorize the words and say them to yourself. Here it is:

I love you. You are precious and special. I want you. I will take care of you. My love will heal. You have nothing to fear. I will be with you always, even in death. You can trust me. You can trust your inner voice. I see, hear, and feel you. I love you completely and forever. I encourage you to explore your uniqueness.

In addition to loving your actions and behavior, I love your light, your essence, the spirit of God in you. I love you and have confidence in you. I know you can do anything you want to do. I will pick you up when you fall. I will set limits and I will enforce them. You are beautiful and I give you permission to be a sexual, loving being. I give you permission to be different from me, all that I am and all that I am not.

The Big Step—Risking Love

Using the Fourth and Fifth POWER Tools, risking and reaching out in love, may be a big step for you if you have a fear of intimacy. You can start out with simple things. Play with a little puppy and enjoy the unconditional love that it gives you. See that no matter how stern a voice you adopt, the puppy comes back to you wagging its tail.

Start hugging other people. We hug wherever we go, and we find that other people really like it. They respond, and we feel loved, too. Dare to tell other people that you love them, that you appreciate them not only for the good things they do for you, but that you love them because they are the persons they are.

Jane still remembers the wonderful experience she had in playing Juliet in her high school production of *Romeo and Juliet*. These star-crossed lovers were prevented from marrying because their families were feuding with each other. "A rose by any other name would smell as sweet," Juliet said of Romeo. Jane believes that many people today, unlike Juliet, let race, class, or religious distinctions prevent them from reaching out to another in love. When you practice *agape* love, you won't think about such differences.

Will others respond? Not always. Just as there are people who cannot give love, there are others who cannot accept it. We believe, however, that the benefits of loving come when you are giving to another.

Once, when Jane was giving a speech in Philadelphia, she saw people protesting Mother Teresa's proposal to build a shelter for the homeless. Here was a beautiful, spiritual person practicing unconditional love and being opposed for it. Did Mother Teresa retaliate? No. She simply smiled, accepted the protesters as they were, and then went on about her business of loving those who needed it the most.

When you can reach out in this way, you will know that you love yourself, that love will spill over, enabling you to give others *agape* love. And that means life for you.

15

Life Plus for You, Too

We started this book with a promise. We told you that even if problems with your children, your marriage, your finances, or your health had you mired in the mud, you could get unstuck. By using the POWER tools, we promised that you could be freed from the prison of your negative thoughts and begin to feel beautiful from the inside out, as well as improve your health, enhance your productivity, and master self-discipline. You could even develop a sense of humor and an appreciation of beauty. When you met your need for a close relationship with God, you would be able to interact peacefully with others. You would know how to give and receive love.

When you had met all these needs, we promised, you could have Life Plus, a quality of living so wonderful that you would never have to feel stuck again.

We knew this was true because we had seen so many people get unstuck and stay that way. Before Bob learned to meet his needs, he had had seven jobs in eight years, had developed agoraphobia, and had even considered suicide. After he found Life Plus, he went through the trauma of a divorce and a major career change, but he did not get stuck. He went on to find happiness that he never would have believed possible.

Jane had felt stuck many times, too. As a child she had been burned and scarred, causing other children to reject her. Then she had cancer. Later, as an adult, she was divorced. After she learned to meet her basic needs, Jane also found Life Plus. Now she has a successful new career, a happy marriage, and the knowledge that she never has to feel stuck again.

If you find Life Plus, does that mean you will never experience failure, disappointment, disease, or loss? Of course not. Just as Bob experienced pain in the aftermath of divorce after he found Life Plus, you also will go through periods when life doesn't go smoothly. The difference is that you *don't have to get or stay stuck*. In the title of this book we use the phrase *Getting* (rather than *Get*) *Unstuck* for a good reason. It is an ongoing *process* rather than a one-time action. Whenever you feel stuck, you can review your ten basic needs, discern which ones you are not fulfilling, use the POWER tools to meet those needs, and then move quickly out of your rut. You can start fresh and achieve more than you thought possible.

When Paul wrote the great affirmation "In everything God works for good with those who love him" (Romans 8:28), he had every reason to feel stuck. He had been jailed, beaten, and rejected because of his faith, yet he wrote, "What shall separate us from the love of Christ? Shall tribulation, or distress, or persecution, or famine, or nakedness, or peril, or sword? . . . No, in all these things we are more than conquerors through him who loved us" (Romans 8:35–37). Paul didn't have to stay stuck because he knew how to center his life on God.

Barriers to Life Plus

As you read our stories, you might have thought, "I'm glad that those terrible things didn't happen to me." If you told us the things that cause *you* to feel stuck, however, we might say the same thing! The fact is that anyone who has lived very long has a story containing elements that are tragic, infuriating, or dehumanizing. Jane's mother grew up in poverty because her father deserted his family of five children. Five of her father's twelve brothers and sisters died as children. One of them was simply working a paper route when a power line fell on him. People at our seminars tell of living through economic depressions, wars, job problems, and business failures; of having physical handicaps, abusive parents or spouses, or children who go astray. We are always amazed at how many can say, "Because of this problem, I am a *better person*." They have found the gift that always lies buried in adversity.

Other people may find nothing but pain and sorrow in these situations, because they are not taking action to get unstuck. When a car falls into a ditch, it stays there until someone hauls it out. A simple law of physics requires that the tow truck that pulls the car out must have more power than the force of gravity that is holding it in the ditch. To overcome inertia, you have to expend a lot of energy. Some people refuse to believe that they have enough energy. They rationalize away the need to put forth effort.

What are some of the statements that pull people down and prevent them from meeting their needs? Take a look at these four big ones and see whether you are standing in your own way:

1. *"It's my cross to bear."* How often have you heard people say this? "I don't have any money, *but* that's just my cross to bear." Or, "My boss treats me terribly, *but* that's just my cross to bear." Or, "I'm too fat," or "I don't get along with my family," or "I have panic attacks, *but* that's just my cross to bear." They may sincerely believe they are submitting to God's will in this way, but actually they are *opposing* it. When Jesus said to take up your cross and follow him, he did not mean to give up and blame everything that goes bad in your life on the cross. He was saying, "Pick up your cross, *even if it is heavy*, and carry it, and I will help you follow me on the path of love, of eternal energy in life, of light, of joy, happiness, productivity, and a wonderful relationship with God."

Because Jim Abbott was born without a right hand, he could have said, "That's just my cross to bear," and decided he couldn't do what other people could. Instead, Jim learned to pitch a baseball *better* than all his friends who had two hands, according to an Associated Press story that was published all over the United States. Jim became the pitcher for the University of Michigan's baseball team. He went on to pitch for Team USA, which in the 1987 Pan American Games beat Cuba in Cuba for the first time in twenty-five years. Team USA received a silver medal, but that wasn't all. In 1988, twenty-year-old Abbott received the prestigious Sullivan Award as the nation's top amateur athlete. It was the first time the Sullivan Award had ever been given to a baseball player.

2. *"I'm trying very hard."* What's wrong with trying? *Trying is lying.* If you don't believe that this is true, *try* to pick up an object that is nearby. Did you pick it up?

That's not what we asked you to do. We asked you to *try* to pick it up. You can't do that, can you? You either pick it up or you don't. Trying gets you nowhere. When you tell yourself how hard you are trying, you are simply reinforcing the thought that the task you want to do is hard or worrisome, even futile. Usually when you say you are *trying* to stay on your diet, or *trying* to study to upgrade your skills, or *trying* to be more loving to someone, it is because you unconsciously think that you cannot do it.

Watch yourself. Every time you use the word *try*, eliminate it. As Bob discovered when he stopped giving in to Mr. Negative, the unconscious is a powerful force for helping or hurting you. If you feed it negative messages like "I'll try," or "I'm not sure I can do what other people do," or "I'd like to be able to do what others do, *but*" it will make sure that you feel uncomfortable with success. Negative words are ways to play the victim. Affirmations are ways to grow.

3. *"I don't have time."* Usually when one of us uses these words, we are saying either, "I don't really want to," or "I'm not going to take the time." It's okay to pick your priorities, but if it is something that you really want to do, you know you can *make the time to do it*. How badly do you want to get unstuck? Do you want growth and happiness more than gloom, depression, frustration, anger, or sadness? If so, set aside one hour a day in which you will work on meeting your needs.

4. *"I don't feel like working to meet my needs."* It is true that when you are stuck you may not feel like setting aside time and expending the necessary energy to meet your needs. You may not even want to take the trouble to write down some goals. But the plain

truth is that you will never *feel* like doing it; and if you never do it, you will never get unstuck.

Take action now, regardless of your feelings, and the feelings will begin to change. *Focus your energy on the solution rather than the problem*, and get unstuck.

From Gateways to Life Plus

Now let's look at four ways you can overcome the inertia of being stuck:

1. *Recognize "what is" rather than "what isn't."* If you are stuck, you may have developed habits of which you are not aware that are keeping you stuck. These habits "feel right" simply because that's the way you've always done things. Now, however, they are keeping you unhappy and stuck. Identifying what is true about yourself may be a shock, but it is a good way to start changing.

When Bob was getting over agoraphobia, he learned that fear was nothing more than a bad habit. He was always telling himself that he couldn't do things as well as other people could and that he was bound to fail. He didn't realize that these negative statements were merely a habit but that every time he fell into this habit, his unconscious received the message that the world was a dangerous place. In order to flee or fight this omnipresent danger, it triggered the release of adrenaline in his bloodstream. The resulting panic attacks only increased Bob's fear and negative thinking.

To change this habit, Bob bought some blue stickers, which he placed on his wristwatch, on a wall in each room of the house, and on the car dashboard. Every time his eye fell on a blue sticker, he asked himself what he was thinking. To his surprise, he was nearly always putting himself down! By identifying his negative think-ing habit, Bob was able to change it.

2. *Replace bad habits with good ones*. If you discover that your "what is" includes bad habits, understand that you don't have to give in to them. You are the master, not your habits. As Bob learned when he discovered that he was a negative thinker, you can break negative habits by putting out effort to develop positive habits instead. Each time Bob found himself putting himself down, for instance, he immediately affirmed that he was beautiful on the inside, that he was a person of worth and that he deserved to do all the things he wanted to do. He made a point of praising one good thing he did each day. Bob used all the POWER tools to break this vicious habit. He meditated and visualized. He risked going out of the house and exposing himself to the situations he feared. He reached out to other agoraphobics. By replacing his bad habits with good ones, he overcame his panic attacks.

3. *Be willing to let go of your resistance to change*. Sometimes you know that you have a bad habit, but going through the discomfort of making changes doesn't seem worthwhile. By setting goals and using the POWER tools, you can overcome this resistance.

Once Jane was feeling stuck, both in her teaching career and in a relationship that caused much pain. She wanted to let go of both and make some positive changes in her life, but somehow she couldn't. No mat-ter how boring her job or how damaging the relation-ship, the uncertainties of making a change were too frightening. Then she attended a seminar for people who wanted to make all kinds of changes, from losing weight and stopping smoking to relaxing their control over their teenagers. The leaders told all the participants to pretend that they held a balloon on a string in each hand. Written on the balloons were descriptions of the changes everyone was afraid to make. Jane visualized the words "I can't change my job" and "I can't let go of this relationship" on her balloons. The leader told everyone to clench their hands around the strings. When it seemed as if their fingers would break, he told them to hold on even tighter. After fifteen minutes, they were in real pain. Then he told them they could let go.

"The strange thing was that even though my fingernails were digging into my palms, I didn't want to let go! I knew that when I first opened my hands, the pain would be even worse than all the clenching. That was the same way I felt about letting go of my teaching job and the disastrous relationship. When I did let go of the balloons, however, the pain quickly went away, and my hands felt relaxed as never before. It was such a wonderful feeling that I realized that even if it hurt to let go of my job and the relationship, the initial discomfort was nothing compared to the rewards waiting for me if I did," Jane says.

If resistance is your problem, set your goals to change, then make good use of the Third POWER Tool. Visualize yourself letting go of the bad habits you are holding so tightly. See yourself practicing new habits, and hold on to them so tightly that the bad ones can never return.

4. *Live in the present moment.* Just as you need to recognize "what is" about yourself, you also need to recognize "what is" about the time you live in. Many people tell themselves, "I'll change tomorrow" or "If only that terrible thing hadn't happened to me, I wouldn't be in this bad situation right now." You cannot

change the past, nor can you predict the future. You can, however, change the odds about whether your future will be happy and fulfilled by what you do today, in the present moment.

Your Six-Point Plan for Finding Life Plus

To be sure that you are living in the present moment, we have devised a six-point plan that you can use to get started on the path to Life Plus. Here it is:

1. Read this book through two times.

2. Do the exercises in chapters 1 through 4 in order to master the POWER tools.

3. Decide which basic human need you will work on first.

4. Set goals to meet your number one need.

5. Follow the directions in the chapter on your number one need to help you meet that need.

6. Use a Daily Monitor to be sure that you are working on your goals daily. To do this, ask yourself questions at regular times during the day to see how much progress you are making in fulfilling your need. Use affirmations to encourage yourself to continue to move forward.

We suggest that you practice your Daily Monitor three times a day: in the morning before you begin your day, at midday to see how you're doing, and at night before bedtime to affirm how well you have done and to ask God to help you with the changes you still need to make.

In the morning, ask yourself, "What action will I take today to work on meeting my needs?" Write your plans in your notebook. Then affirm that you are a worthy person who deserves to meet your needs. Ask God to help you take the risks you must take to fulfill these needs.

At noon, ask yourself the following questions:

- Have I taken the action that I planned to take today to meet my needs, or have I made firm plans to do so?
- Have I asked God to help me meet my needs today?
- Have I visualized and affirmed a positive outcome for meeting my needs?

In the evening, ask yourself:

- What action did I take today to meet my needs?
- Have I believed that I deserved to meet these needs?
- Have I written in my journal today?
- Have I given myself "Attaboys" or "Attagirls" for every attempt I have made to change myself, regardless of the outcome?

You may also want to use a Two-Month Monitor to check your progress. Ask yourself the following questions, and write your answers in your journal.

- What progress have I made in the past two months?
- Have I rewarded myself for this progress? If not, what treat will I give myself today?
- In what areas have I progressed less than I had hoped?
- What new goals will help me progress?
- How will I carry out these goals?

• Have I used my progress in any way to help others meet their needs?

Is Life Plus Really for You?

You may be wondering how you will find enough energy to get unstuck from an unhappy marriage, an unsatisfactory job, frustrations with your children, or any of the other million ways to feel stuck.

If it doesn't seem possible for you, consider the men and women whom we profiled in this book, as well as those in the Bible, who got unstuck because *they made a decision*.

What about Peter, who toiled all night without catching any fish (Luke 5:3–8)? As he sat in his boat on Lake Gennesaret, discouraged with his empty nets, he had every reason to feel stuck. Then Jesus told him to cast his nets into the sea one more time. When he did, his boat almost sank because the catch was so great.

Even though he wanted to quit, Peter had enough faith to try just one more time, and through that brave faith he received a miracle that made up for all the other failures. Peter didn't sit back and wait for more miracles to occur. Then and there he made a decision to follow Jesus, and he became the most impressive "fisher of men" of all the apostles. Because he trusted his own strength and faith, he was never really stuck again—even though he later disappointed himself by denying Jesus three times and even when he himself endured persecution.

And what about the unnamed woman who was a prostitute until Jesus told her, "You don't have to be stuck that way any more. You can stop being a prostitute. And I love you." Was that woman Mary Magdalene, from whom Jesus cast out seven demons (Mark

16:9)? Or were Mary's "evil spirits and infirmities" a description of poor health or some other form of being stuck? We do not know for sure, but we do know that once Mary Magdalene met Jesus, she was never stuck again. She experienced anguish and suffering at the crucifixion, but she went on to become the first witness to the resurrection.

And what about Matthew, the wealthy tax collector who knew that he was hated because he cheated everyone (Matthew 9:9)? As he sat at his desk counting his money, was Matthew thinking, "Is this all there is?" All we know is that when Jesus said, "Follow me," Matthew did. That very night he reached out to others who were stuck, inviting them to a feast where they could meet Jesus for themselves.

What about you? Will you stay stuck? Or will you make the decision to step out, meet your needs, and find Life Plus? We know you can do it, and that God extends his hand in help and love. We urge you to accept all the happiness, joy, peace, and accomplishments that are waiting for you.

Bibliography

ASH, MARY KAY. *Mary Kay*. New York: Harper and Row, 1981.

BELL, MARTIN. *The Way of the Wolf*. New York: Ballantine, 1968.

BLANCHARD, KEN. *The One Minute Manager*. New York: William Morrow, 1982.

BRADSHAW, JOHN. *On the Family*. Pompano Beach, Florida: Health Communications, Inc., 1988.

BROWN, PETER, AND GAINES, STEVEN. *The Love You Make, an Insider's Story of the Beatles*. New York: McGraw-Hill, 1983.

COHEN, ALAN. *Rising in Love*. Farmingdale, New York: Coleman Graphics, 1983.

COOPER, KENNETH. *Aerobics*. New York: M. Evans, Co., 1968.

COUSINS, NORMAN. *Anatomy of an Illness as Perceived by the Patient*. New York: W. W. Norton & Co., 1979.

CROWLEY, MARY. *You Can Too*. Old Tappan, New Jersey: Fleming H. Revell, 1976

CURTIS, DONALD. *Your Thoughts Can Change Your Life*. New York: Prentice Hall, 1961.

———. *Human Problems and How to Solve Them*. New York: Prentice Hall, 1974.

———. *Daily Power for Joyful Living*. New York: Prentice Hall, 1974.

EARECKSON, JONI, WITH MUSSER, JOE. *Joni*. New York: Bantam, 1978.

FOLLETT, KEN. *On Wings of Eagles*. New York: William Morrow and Co., Inc., 1983.

GIBRAN, KAHLIL. *The Prophet*. New York: Alfred Knopf, 1969.

GODDARD, JOHN. *Kayaks Down the Nile*. Salt Lake City: Brigham Young University Press, 1979.

GAMBRELL, HERBERT P. *A Pictorial History of Texas*. E. P. Dutton, 1960.

GARFIELD, CHARLES. *Peak Performance*. New York: Warner, 1985.

GAWAIN, SHAKTI. *Creative Visualization*. South Holland, Illinois: Bantam New Age, 1979.

GORDON, DR. THOMAS. *Parent Effectiveness Training*. New York: Peter H. Wyden, Inc., 1970.

HAMMERSCHLAG, CARL A., M.D. *The Dancing Healers*. New York: Harper and Row, 1988.

HILL, NAPOLEON. *Think and Grow Rich*. New York: Fawcett Press, 1960.

HURT, HARRY, III. *Texas Rich*. New York: W. W. Norton & Co., 1981.

LEONARD, GEORGE B. *Transformation*. Los Angeles: J. P. Tarcher, Inc., 1972.

LINKLETTER, ART. *Drugs at my Doorstep*. Waco, Texas: Word Publishing, 1973.

MALTZ, MAXWELL, M.D. *Psychocybernetics*. New York: Prentice Hall, 1960.

MANDINO, OG. *The Greatest Salesman in the World*. New York: Bantam, 1974.

———. *The Greatest Salesman in the World, Part II*. New York: Bantam, 1988.

MCCULLOUGH, CHRISTOPHER J., PH.D. *Managing Your Anxiety*. Los Angeles: J. P. Tarcher, Inc., 1985.

MURRAY, WILLIAM J. *My Life Without God*. Nashville: Thomas Nelson, 1982.

NEFF, PAULINE. *Tough Love*. Nashville: Abingdon, 1982.

PEALE, NORMAN VINCENT. *Dynamic Imaging*. Old Tappan, New Jersey: Fleming H. Revell, 1982.

PECK, M. SCOTT, M.D. *The Road Less Traveled*. New York: Simon and Schuster, 1978.

POWELL, JOHN. *The Secret of Staying in Love*. Niles, Illinois: Argus Communications, 1974.

RIDER, MARK. "Treating Chronic Disease and Pain with Music-Mediated Imagery." *The Arts in Psychotherapy*, 1987.

RUBENSTEIN, CARIN, PH.D., AND SHAVER, PHILLIP, PH.D. *In Search of Intimacy*. New York: Delacorte Press, 1982.

SCHULLER, ROBERT. *Tough Times Never Last but Tough People Do*. Nashville: Thomas Nelson, 1983.

WEBER, BILL. *Conquering the Kill Joys*. Waco, Texas: Word Books, 1986.

WILSON, R. REID, PH.D. *Don't Panic*. New York: Harper and Row, 1986.

ZIGLAR, ZIG. *See You at the Top*. Gretna, Louisiana: Pelican Publishing Co., 1983.

ZAHODY, JOHN PAUL. *The Secret of Staying Together*. Altadena, California: Heartlight Publications, 1985.

Index

About the Authors

Through their Dallas-based company Life Plus, JANE and ROBERT HANDLY conduct programs helping thousands of people in Fortune 500 companies, associations, and religious groups achieve goals, attain peak performance, reduce stress, and enrich life. They have appeared on "Phil Donahue," "Nightline," Dr. Robert Schuller's "Hour of Power," and many other shows. They are members of the National Speakers Association, and both have served as president of the North Texas Speakers Association. They live in Dallas, Texas.

Dallas writer Pauline Neff was coauthor with Robert Handly of *Anxiety & Panic Attacks: Their Cause and Cure*, and *Beyond Fear*. She was also the author of *Tough Love*.

SELF
HELP
from
FAWCETT